Spearfishing and Underwater Hunting Handbook

Beginner through Advanced

By
B. Allen Patrick

Copyright 1996

Active Adventure Publishing
St. Petersburg, Florida

Spearfishing and Underwater Hunting Handbook
Beginner through Advanced

Copyright © 1996 by
Active Adventure Publishing
701 94th Avenue N., Suite 104
St. Petersburg, FL 33702
(813)827-0349; FAX: (813)578-3000
email: actadvent@aol.com

Library of Congress Catalog Card Number: 96-79542

B. Allen Patrick
Spearfishing and Underwater Hunting Handbook
Beginner through Advanced

Published in 1996 by Active Adventure Publishing, St. Petersburg, Florida
Spearfishing: Sport, Art, and Technique.
1. Skin Diving, 2. Spearfishing. 3. Fishing.

International Standard Book Number: 1-890079-11-1

Printed in the United States of America

Dedicated To

Bonnie (Patrick) Gross, who, though she could hardly swim a lick, had the courage and wisdom to let her son pursue his passion for the water.

Acknowledgments

This book was made possible by the contributions of members of the **St. Petersburg Underwater Club (SPUC), Sunshine Fins Dive Club, Florida Skin Divers Association**, and the sport diving community.

Special thanks to **Jim Zumwalt, Lex Ballantyne**, and **Gordon Reyher** for their editorial guidance and contributions to content.

Cover photography courtesy of **Denny Iwago, Jamie Joanos**, and **Jim Zumwalt**. Additional photography credit goes to **Denny Iwago, Cathy Carey, Mark Frisbie, Jamie Joanos, Jerry Rice**, and **Jim Zumwalt**. The distributors and manufacturers receive citations of credit throughout the book for providing their equipment photographs and diagrams.

An extra special thanks goes to **Elaine Patrick** for her help on the cover and for putting up with my long and late hours.

In addition, the following individuals contributed their greatly appreciated advise, proof reading and editorial assistance, use of equipment and facilities, photographs, and much needed encouragement:

Nick Anderson
Ditmar Biller
Lou Bonsey
Kevin Bruington
Wayne Butts
Cathy Carey
Steve Cody
Dan Curran
Ned Deloach
Valerie Daubert
Jackie Draffin
Wendell Fountain

David & Stephanie Frank
Bill Hardman
Robby Hassan
Carl Holland
Denny Iwago
Jamie Joanos
Paul Jones
Paul Kerr
Lt. Col. Ray B. May
Paul Renner
Frank & Becky Rhodes

Table of Contents

This section represents the initial installment of a continuing forum on underwater hunting topics. These first two topics cover lobstering and scalloping as practiced in Florida. Additional underwater hunting publications and updates on spearfishing itself are planned for the future. Send in the post card from the back of this book to receive notices of upcoming articles. (Your name and address will only be used by Active Adventure Publishing and not released to the junk mail generators.)

Specialty Underwater Hunting -- Lobstering
In the search for delectable goodies from the sea, few treats top the taste of lobster. This installment describes hunting, cleaning, and preparing Florida Spiny Lobster.

Specialty Underwater Hunting -- Scalloping
Atlantic blue-eyed bay scallops, also found in the Gulf of Mexico, provide a great meal. Hunting them is addictive and the shallow freediving required to collect them improves your snorkeling skill. This installment of Specialty Underwater Hunting tells how to find, collect, clean, and prepare bay scallops.

Spearfishing is a controversial diving specialty. This section presents spearfishing as the most selective and least wasteful method of harvesting from the sea.

This section lists manufacturers of spearfishing equipment. If you have difficulty locating a piece of equipment, check with one of these companies.

Understanding a subject depends upon understanding its jargon (fancy word for slang). The Glossary would have been placed at the beginning of the book if it weren't so boring. You may want to scan it first to prepare for some of the spearfishing terms and definitions.

SPEARFISHING AND UNDERWATER HUNTING thoroughly covers spearfishing technique and equipment. However, general dive related topics are addressed in more detail by other sources. Refer to the Bibliography for a list of recommended sources on such topics as history, physics, diving equipment and technique, fish identification, dive computers and dive table theory, and site location. The bibliography also lists several magazine articles and video tapes related to spearfishing and underwater hunting.

Introduction

Exciting, exhilarating, and at times frustrating, underwater hunting enhances the thrill of skin and scuba diving. It combines the excitement of diving under the surface of the world's oceans, lakes, and rivers with the challenge of hunting. In addition, it rewards your effort with fresh seafood.

For whom is *Spearfishing And Underwater Hunting Handbook* intended? For divers new to spearfishing, it introduces spearfishing and hunting technique in a "how to" format. For experienced underwater hunters, it serves as a spearfishing equipment and technique reference. *Spearfishing and Underwater Hunting Handbook* reveals tips and secrets (until now anyway) of some of the best underwater hunters in the country.

The author's writing style is informal yet to the point. Each chapter presents objectives at the beginning and review questions at the end. This provides a convenient format for using *Spearfishing and Underwater Hunting Handbook* as a learning and reference aid in spearfishing and underwater hunting specialty courses. **HOWEVER.... This book is not intended as a replacement of spearfishing or diving training.**

The term "spearfisherman" or other implicit references may seem to indicate that spearfishing is a sport for men. Not so! Some of the best underwater hunters are women. Any reference to man, men, he, his, him, etceteras is intended only to help the wording flow smoothly. Some lady spearfisherpersons are better than this author will ever be. So, please accept this gender-specific, perhaps "politically incorrect" writing style for its simplicity.

Emphasis centers on function and technique. There are photographs but not all of them depict equipment fresh off the assembly line. To illustrate gun configurations some illustrative photographs show working spearguns that have been "around the ledge a time or two." There are photographs of new equipment but the primary intent for illustrations is function, not image. Like a Browning® shotgun or Weatherby® rifle, some spearguns are a work of art and an object of pride for their owners. Others are "pickup truck, get the job done" tools of the sport.

When discussing general topics like basic skills, safety, and ethics, the term "speargun" is used generically to refer to all types of spear delivery systems. This includes spearguns, Hawaiian slings, pole spears, and gigs. When needed, the book distinguishes between the various spear delivery systems.

The book presents historical information sparingly. Spearfishing attracted many diving pioneers to the sport. Early Man probably used sharp sticks to spear fish from the surface. However, this is a "how it's done now" book. Unless it relates to current spearfishing technique, discussions omit spearfishing history. Refer to the bibliography for sources on history and additional spearfishing related topics.

Now, Let's get on with the real reason you are reading this book!

Chapter 1: Diving Skill and Experience

Introduction

Before taking up spearfishing a diver should possess at least an intermediate level of diving expertise. Intermediate skill refers more to a diver's ability and comfort in the water than it does to "passing" a certain certification level. This chapter provides a guideline for assessing your skill before taking up spearfishing.

Spearfishing, like diving in general, is safe when its special rules are followed. Part of following diving rules means being prepared, skilled, and in adequate physical condition for the type of diving activity pursued. Most of this chapter focuses on prerequisite scuba skills for spearfishing. As with beginning the sport of diving itself, you should consult a diving physician for assurance that you are physically capable of pursuing this sport.

Breath hold diving, also known as freediving or apnea diving, enjoys popularity in spearfishing. The last part of this chapter addresses freediving.

Note: Spearfishing while using surface supplied air, also referred to as "hookah" rig diving, is not discussed separately. Consider the skills for spearfishing while using surface supplied air comparable to diving with scuba. The same rules for breathing air at depth and other safe diving practices apply. However, surface supplied air differs from scuba in that there is no submersible pressure gauge and there is an "umbilical" air hose leading to the surface. The umbilical restricts a diver's ability to pursue fish and increases potential for entanglement.

Objectives
By the end of this section you should be able to:
1. Explain why a spearfisherman should have an intermediate skill level before taking up spearfishing.
2. List the basic and advanced skills that are important in spearfishing and why they are important.
3. Describe the fitness level needed before taking up spearfishing.
4. Describe freediving or apnea diving.
5. Describe shallow water blackout as it relates to freediving.

General Considerations
"OK, I'm a certified diver. What's next?"

Newly certified divers typically satisfy themselves by just diving. They enjoy the challenge of becoming more skilled and comfortable in the water. The thrill of being underwater and taking in the visions of an almost alien world of strange marine life captivates them. For many divers this sheer enjoyment provides plenty of excitement, but in time most divers look for something else. They begin to consider various specialties and look for more challenging ways to apply their newly acquired diving skill.

Some take up diving specialties such as photography, shell and fossil collecting, cave or wreck diving, mixed gas diving, tropical fish collecting, or other underwater "hobbies". Diving specialties are not mutually exclusive. A diver often maintains an interest in several specialties. Some divers, driven perhaps by a primal hunting instinct or maybe a love for fresh fish, take up spearfishing.

Spearfishing represents but one of the specialties that divers branch into and one that requires an intermediate level of diving expertise to assure composure, judgment, and safety. Before taking up spearfishing a diver's skill must be second nature. Taking up other specialties before taking up spearfishing helps hone a diver's skill. Non-spearfishing diving specialties provide an opportunity to become comfortable "working" underwater. Underwater photography, in particular, helps teach buoyancy control, stalking, and aiming skills, which are also important in spearfishing.

Why recommend a "second nature" skill level? A spearfisherman must be responsible. His safety, the safety of other divers, and the safety of the environment depend upon it. A spearfisherman must always remain aware of his actions and the potential dangers involved in spearfishing.

Spearguns function like firearms and demand safe handling. They should be pointed in a harmless direction unless targeting a fish. A diver who is preoccupied by the need to concentrate on basic diving technique can not focus proper respect on his speargun. Just as a hunter does not need to concentrate on walking technique in the woods, a spearfisherman must feel the same comfort level with diving. Spearfishing safety in itself encompasses a separate subject and receives more detailed attention in **Chapter 7: Spearfishing Safety**; however, a sufficient diving skill level will ensure that a diver can concentrate on spearfishing.

"OK! OK! How do I know if I have this skill level? I've been walking a long time. Don't even remember learning. But diving.... I just got certified a while back. How do I know....?"

Fortunately, we are in the age of structured training and certification. Name a recreational activity, such as rollerblading, snow skiing, sailing, etc., and you will find training programs available for it. The diving industry in particular makes training available to ensure that divers learn the skills necessary to dive safely and grow their skill. Spearfishing or underwater hunter specialty courses provide ideal paths for learning to spearfish. Instructors can help you assess your skill level.

"How do I find a spearfishing or underwater hunter course?"

Find a dive center that caters to spearfishermen. You can recognize these centers by their good supply of spearfishing equipment and bulletin boards filled with photographs of recent spearfishing catches. In addition, stores catering to spearfishermen usually offer spearfishing dive charter trips to help you gain experience after completing their course.

When choosing a spearfishing course insist upon professionalism. A good spearfisherman does not necessarily make a good spearfishing teacher! Professional sports is filled with great players, but few of them make good coaches. Some of the best coaches were not necessarily great players. Look for an instructor who teaches and doesn't just tell spearfishing "war stories." Spearfishing stories provide entertainment and can be instructional, but stories should not replace solid instruction and two-way communication!

Look for instructors and center staff who want to help you learn and understand. Avoid those who talk down to you or try to intimidate you with their knowledge. (If you are a psychologist maybe try to sell those types some of your services.) Look for an instructor whose eyes light up when he talks with you about spearfishing. He (Remember in this book, "he" can mean "she") should take a genuine interest in your learning.

As previously mentioned, a diver should possess an intermediate skill level before taking up spearfishing. Training facilities will have their own prerequisite skill requirements for various specialty classes. Some certifying agencies require only a basic open water rating before enrolling in an underwater hunter course. This is fine if the underwater hunter course concentrates on collecting scallops, lobster, or abalone; however, an intermediate skill level is recommended for spearfishing. This ensures that you are comfortable in the water prior to taking on the responsibility of diving with a speargun.

"So, what does "intermediate skill level" mean?"

Possessing an advanced dive card is an indicator of experience, not necessarily skill. Possessing skill is more important than having an advanced certification card. However, the advanced certification rating usually indicates that a diver is ready for spearfishing. Advanced certification holders usually possess the following skills and experience:

- Basic diving skills: Familiarity with diving equipment, mastery of basic water skills, including exceptional buoyancy control, and dive table proficiency;
- Advanced diving skills: Underwater navigation, fish identification, and fifteen-plus logged dives within the past year.

Basic Diving Skills

To complete a basic open water scuba course a student must demonstrate certain skills. For an intermediate level, "self-reliant" diver the ability to perform basic skills comes automatically. After fifteen or so dives such tasks as breathing continuously, ear and sinus equalization, mask clearing, swimming effectively, and gearing up should pose little challenge. Other skills, such as underwater mask removal and replacement and buoyancy control, may not have been practiced regularly. These and other skills need to be emphasized for spearfishing.

Eventually, you will perform underwater mask removal, replacement, and clearing in an actual diving situation. Either an errant fin from a fellow diver, a surging anchor line, clumsy entry, or other unplanned event will knock off your mask. Having your hands full of spearfishing equipment and, hopefully, a stringer of fish makes mask replacement more challenging. But, with preparation and practice you will succeed in replacing and clearing your mask. Before taking up spearfishing become accomplished at replacing and clearing your mask while carrying other equipment.

Effective buoyancy control distinguishes an accomplished diver from an inexperienced one. Proper buoyancy control allows a diver to glide gracefully among his underwater surroundings. Calm, smooth motion will result in more effective spearfishing. Maintaining proper buoyancy throughout a dive also reduces effort, which in turn reduces fatigue and air consumption.

What makes buoyancy control challenging? Buoyancy changes during a dive. It varies primarily as a result of physical changes to a diver's gear. As his scuba cylinder empties it becomes more buoyant. Wet suits provide more buoyancy near the surface but become less buoyant as trapped air spaces collapse and air escapes during a dive. Weight yourself properly to compensate for these changes.

Changes in cylinder buoyancy exert the most dramatic effect toward the end of a dive. You may "pass" the neutral buoyancy test prior to a dive but find yourself buoyant while on a 15 foot safety stop at the end of the dive. The classic neutral buoyancy test consists of floating at eye level with your lungs half full of air and no air in your bcd. With tank pressure down to 500 psi and no air in your bcd, hovering can prove difficult. Compensating for poor buoyancy control by sculling or "finning" with your hands will be awkward while holding spearfishing gear and fish. To avoid this clumsy situation compensate for changing tank buoyancy, by adding approximately three pounds more weight than the classic neutral buoyancy test indicates.

Besides the extra hand carried gear, fish carried on a stringer introduce additional buoyancy complications due to their swim bladders. **Chapter 6: Technique** addresses this situation.

The need to monitor air consumption by regularly checking your submersible pressure gauge should come as second nature prior to taking up spearfishing. The term "self-reliant diver" appeared earlier. A self-reliant diver takes responsibility for setting up his own gear, monitoring his own air consumption, and diving with minimal help.

Many divers dive with a divemaster who regularly reminds them to check air pressure and determines when everyone will ascend. When you begin spearfishing you typically do not dive with a divemaster. You dive with a buddy with whom you share equal responsibility for safety. Learn to work as a buddy team. Establish a habit of checking your air throughout a dive, not just near what you think is the end of the dive. Occasionally, show your buddy how much air you have remaining and check his remaining air. By doing this you both will have an idea of how much longer the dive will last. This also helps avoid a "low on air situation." Due to the excitement of the sport, unexpectedly high air consumption while spearfishing sometimes surprises even experienced divers. Remember the buddy system and watch your air.

It is also easy to lose track of depth and time when spearfishing. Along with checking air consumption on a regular basis, monitor depth and time. The basic rule of "Plan Your Dive; Dive Your Plan" needs to be underscored for spearfishing. Avoid the temptation to follow an elusive fish a little deeper or waiting a little longer for him to come out from under that ledge. He will be down there next time. Return to the surface and come back later.

Part of self-reliance means not trusting one piece of equipment too much. Divers can somehow tune out audible alarms on computers and watches when taunted by a challenging fish. Wouldn't it be an unpleasant surprise to overstay your bottom time because you didn't hear an alarm? Frequently perform your own visual air, depth, and time monitoring.

Not all dive sites hold "quarry" fish. As a result, spearfishing typically involves more dives during a day than typical sightseeing dives. A group of spearfishermen may make several dives with each dive of relatively short duration. This requires careful dive planning and management.

Planning dives using dive tables represents a basic diving skill. Prospective spearfishermen need to know the dive tables thoroughly. They particularly need confidence in planning no decompression stop repetitive dives. They need to conservatively adhere to planned depth and bottom time limits during each dive.

Dive computers provide an alternate method for planning repetitive dives. Many scuba spearfishermen use computers. Computers combine the functions of a depth gauge and dive timer into one unit. These devices use dive depth and time history to compute the no-decompression stop time limit at current depth. Between dives they display allowable no-decompression stop bottom times for various depths based upon repetitive dive history and surface interval. Computers offer additional features that vary among models. However, they help eliminate human error in calculating dive plans.

Remember, no computer or dive planning table guarantees to prevent decompression sickness. Plan your dives conservatively and make minimum three minute, fifteen foot safety stops after each one. For more explanation on dive planning tools refer to *Dive Computers, A Consumer's Guide to History, Theory, and Performance*, *Decompression Theory, Dive, Tables, and Dive Computers*, and the *PADI Encyclopedia of Recreational Diving*.

Continuous breathing becomes ingrained with experienced scuba divers. "Never hold your breath" is rule number one in scuba diving and it deserves special attention when spearfishing. Just as the excitement of hunting can distract a diver from monitoring air, depth, and time, excitement can distract a diver from breathing continuously. Besides serving as a safe diving practice, deep, steady breathing also improves spearfishing effectiveness. Deliberate deep breathing, but not hyperventilating, helps reduce excitement and helps avoid "buck fever". Buck fever, as it relates to spearfishing, is the tendency for a diver to be unable to pull the trigger or to miss an easy shot due to over excitement. Continuous breathing is mandatory while scuba diving. Remind yourself before each dive to breath calmly and continuously. It will increase the probability that you will not miss a good fish.

Advanced Diving Skills

An intermediate diver possesses advanced underwater navigation skill and navigation ranks highly in importance for safe and effective spearfishing. Spearfishing often takes place under less than ideal conditions. This makes navigation a challenge. Basic open water classes teach elementary navigation. Advanced certification provided by most agencies places strong emphasis on navigation. Prior to taking up spearfishing sharpen your navigation skill. Finding the dive spot and getting back to the boat are obviously important with any diving activity. Stalking a fish while spearfishing adds a "Will-O-The-Wisp" aspect to navigation. After following a fish for several minutes, a you can find yourself not knowing which direction is which unless you consistently apply good navigation technique.

CPR and first aid training represent good skills for spearfishing and for any outdoor activity. Because spearfishing activity often takes place "off the beaten path" of diving, prepare to cope with basic first aid emergencies by becoming certified in CPR and first aid. Courses offered by the American Red Cross in both CPR and Standard First Aid fulfill this requirement. Some dive training agencies also offer nationally recognized CPR and first aid courses.

The "fifteen-plus logged dives" recommendation stands as a guideline. Some divers need more, some less dives to iron out the wrinkles of learning to dive under control. Most spearfishing course instructors will gladly review your experience with you. They can help you determine your skill level and identify skills that need work. Ask yourself; "Would I want to be in the water (or would I want my loved one in the water) along with me and a speargun?" That sounds like, "Would I belong to a club that would have me as a member?" logic, but be honest in your answer.

Other Recommended Skills

Review your non-spearfishing diving experience and compare it to the type of diving required for spearfishing in your area. Perhaps most of your diving has been from large boats, in pristine clear water, and with groups of divers closely supervised by a divemaster. On the other hand, spearfishing in your area probably involves small boats, with less formal supervision, and in limited visibility conditions. Look for a spearfishing specialty course that gives you the opportunity to dive under characteristic local spearfishing conditions.

"But, I'm not an athlete! How can I take up spearfishing?"

When it comes to fitness, a spearfisherman needs to be fit enough to pass the swim and physical requirements of a basic scuba course. Re-test yourself using the swim requirements from your open water text and confer with your doctor. If you are fit enough to dive, you are fit enough to spearfish. The higher your fitness level the more aggressively you can pursue the spearfishing. Proceed at the pace indicated by your fitness level.

One under-emphasized technique in spearfishing is: Take your time! The fish can out swim you regardless of your athletic ability. You will spook them by racing around. Relax, enjoy the sport, and take your time. It will make you a better spearfisherman.

Spearfishing requires the ability to identify fish and judge their size underwater. Some species of fish are illegal to take and size and possession limits exist for others. The ability to identify fish and know the limits before taking up the sport will help avoid trouble. Spearfishing and underwater hunter specialty courses typically include fish identification training. Learning the common species before beginning the course will give you an advantage during the course. Rules change. Monitor changes in local, state, and federal fishing regulations. Good reference information sources for fish identification include:

- Pamphlets from state and federal fishery, game, and wildlife commissions and agencies;
- *The Dictionary of Fishes*, from Great Outdoors Publishing, is an excellent and inexpensive fish reference;
- *Waterproof Guide to Corals and Fishes*, Seahawk Press Publishing,(available from many dive centers);
- Various waterproof fish identification tables, Seahawk Press Publishing, (available at many dive centers);
- *Audubon Society Field Guide to North American Fishes*, Whales, and Dolphins, from Alfred A. Knof, Inc. publishing;
- *Fishes of the World*, MacMillan Publishing Col, Inc.;
- Specialty courses on fish identification are available from various certifying agencies.

Freediving

Just add mask, fins, snorkel, and speargun (maybe a wetsuit or weight belt) and there you have it -- freedive spearfishing. Freedive spearfishing can be performed at the surface or by holding your breath and making shallow dives. However, some freedivers spearfish at depths below 100 feet. Freedive spearfishing represents the simplest, yet most challenging form of spearfishing.

Some spearfishermen consider freediving, also known as breath hold or apnea diving, as the most sportsman-like way to spearfish. The earliest spearfishermen were freedivers. Many built their own dive gear, such as:

- Masks with copper or inner tube skirts,
- Fins made from tennis shoes with planks attached,
- Crude hand gigs,
- Spearguns employing home made trigger mechanisms.

Early divers did not even use snorkels! Carlos Eyles's book, *The Last of the Blue Water Hunters,* shares some of the exploits of these spearfishing pioneers. It provides interesting reading for anyone pursuing the sport of freediving or spearfishing.

Some governments, for example the Bahamas, allow only freediving when spearfishing. Therefore, full enjoyment of spearfishing requires a certain degree of freediving skill.

Freediving is simple in concept. Take a deep breath, hold it then dive. A tuck or pike dive will help you glide to depth. Perform ear and sinus pressure equalization, commonly referred to as "ear clearing", in the same manner as for scuba diving. Swallow or pinch your nose and exhale lightly as you descend. Upon ascent, clear your snorkel using either the blast or displacement method. Various classes, available through certification agencies and at dive centers, provide training for snorkeling. They teach basic technique but practice builds skill and endurance.

While simple in equipment and concept, the requirements for control, safety, and judgment remain the same. A freediver must accept responsibility for the safety of himself, other divers (or swimmers), and the environment. Just as for scuba divers, underwater hunting specialty courses promote safe diving along with safe spearfishing practices.

Despite its simplicity, freediving carries a unique risk which is commonly referred to as shallow water blackout. Shallow water blackout results in a diver losing consciousness and possibly dying while surfacing from a freedive. The prevailing theory sites the following contributing causes:

- Hyperventilation prior to a dive;
- Carbon dioxide (CO_2) buildup during a dive;
- A reduction of the partial pressure of oxygen as a diver ascends.

Hyperventilation, the rapid inhaling and exhaling of several deep breaths of air before a dive, "blows off" extra amounts of CO_2 from the blood stream. Excess CO_2, not lack of oxygen, in the blood stream serves as the primary trigger for the feeling of the need to breathe. Blowing off excess CO_2 causes the diver to falsely feel that he does not need to breathe. At depth oxygen supply is sufficient due to the increased relative pressure of oxygen within the diver's lungs as compared to that in the blood. As the diver ascends pressure drops and the relative pressure of oxygen within the lungs falls below the critical level. This reduction in oxygen pressure brought on by a lack of a sense for the need to breathe is believed to cause loss of consciousness.

This is a very elementary explanation of the theory of shallow water blackout. Its exact cause remains unknown. Refer to *The Encyclopedia of Recreational Diving* and various other dive texts for a more thorough explanation.

While shallow water blackout causes concern for freedivers, proper technique reduces risk. Experienced freedivers dive in pairs, with one diver on the surface watching the other. Diving in pairs helps guard, but does not provide complete assurance, against death from shallow water blackout. Avoiding hyperventilating by taking no more than three deep breaths before a dive is believed to reduce the possibility of shallow water blackout. Some freedivers advocate diving to depths less than fifty feet to further reduce risk. Fatigue and poor hydration may also contribute to causing shallow water blackout.

The danger is real but occurrences of shallow water blackout are rare. The US Navy discourages its divers from freediving even when off duty. If you are considering spearfishing by freediving study the danger before deciding to freedive.

Even after considering the risk of shallow water blackout, many spearfishermen enjoy freediving. Freediving stands as a matter of pride with divers who consider it spearfishing's purest form and would not spearfish any other way. Everyone must make their own decision. The comments on shallow water blackout are not intended as an indictment against freediving, but to point out the risk. There are too many laws on the books where government interferes with our right to decide. If you decide to freedive, dive safely!

Summary

Spearfishing requires that you possess a competent level of diving skill and experience. Learn spearfishing basics in a underwater hunting specialty course. Then practice those skills and emulate experienced spearfishermen. After reviewing the skills outlined above, confer with a spearfishing instructor and work on weak areas. Spearfishing provides enjoyment from the moment you begin the sport; becoming good at spearfishing takes study and practice.

Review Questions:
1. Why is it necessary for a diver to be self reliant before taking up spearfishing?
2. List five basic skills required for spearfishing on scuba.
3. List two advanced skills recommended for spearfishing.
4. T/F A diver must be a conditioned athlete before taking up spearfishing?
5. What is freediving or apnea diving?
6. What is shallow water blackout?
7. How can risk from shallow water blackout be reduced?

Chapter 2: Dive Gear Considerations

Introduction

Many styles and variations of dive equipment exist on the market. By the time you consider taking up spearfishing you will probably already own basic dive gear with which you feel comfortable. This chapter points out some key considerations in selecting dive equipment for spearfishing. For more detailed information about dive equipment refer to books like *Encyclopedia of Recreational Diving*. Bottom line: Dive with gear you like and with which you feel comfortable.

Objectives
By the end of this section you should be able to:
1. Know the overall consideration in basic gear choice for use in spearfishing.
2. Be able to identify three features of choosing a mask for use in spearfishing.
3. Understand why a mask with a black skirt or a skirt of a color that prevents light from entering from the side is desirable when spearfishing.
4. Know the considerations when selecting fins for use in spearfishing.
5. Understand the pros and cons of various snorkel features.
6. Know the considerations in choosing a bcd for use in spearfishing.
7. Know the features to look for in a regulator used for spearfishing.
8. Understand the pros and cons of the three types of primary weighting systems.
9. List five pieces of miscellaneous gear useful in spearfishing.

Mask

A good mask should: 1) Fit comfortably; 2) Seal well; and, 3) Not fog. Silicone masks tend to last longer than black rubber. Purge valves sometimes get trash in them, causing leaks. High volume or low volume does not matter that much. High volume masks seem less prone to fogging. (Don't ask me to defend that statement...just personal observation.) Low volume masks require less air to equalize with ambient pressure and are particularly popular with freedivers. A wide field of vision is good. Just as a baseball cap cuts down glare, a mask with a black skirt or color that prevents light from entering the mask through the sides will improve vision underwater.

Fins

Fin technology offers a wide variety of designs, many aimed at reducing leg fatigue and increasing efficiency. Some spearfishermen use extra long fins. Others prefer more traditional designs. Research the fin market and buy a style with which you feel most comfortable. If you are strong and dive regularly you will probably want a fin with a larger, stiffer blade design. If you dive less often, tend to cramp or just do not want to kick hard, a smaller, a more flexible bladed fin will probably suit you better.

As far as full foot or strap fins, that depends upon the diving environment and, again, just plain personal preference. Strap fins work better for cold water, when you need to wear booties for warmth. Booties also provide foot protection when walking around on shore or on a boat. Full foot fins, due to their streamlined, tight fit, create less drag and turbulence, tend to wobble less when kicking, and present no entangling straps.

Some divers tape their fin straps to prevent the adjustment from slipping and help prevent them from becoming entangled. If you chose strap fins, carry spare straps.

Many freedivers and some scuba divers prefer super long blade fins. These fins require a longer, slower leg stroke than traditional length fins but provide a smooth, gliding dive. This seems to help conserve energy. One drawback; Long fins present a challenge when diving from a crowded boat or at a crowded dive site. (As you will read in the discussion on safety, you would not be spearfishing in a crowded dive site anyway...right?)

Bottom line: Choose a fin that fits comfortably and provides optimal propulsion with minimum fatigue. Many dive centers will let you try out a style of fin before purchasing. Another way to try out a pair of fins is to borrow a pair from a friend. Whatever you decide upon will probably work better than planks attached to tennis shoes.

Snorkel

With snorkels and spearfishing, simpler is better! Dive gear manufacturers and dive centers sell some very large bore, "dry", purge valve models; however, look for a snorkel with as little drag as possible. Purge valves get trash in them, tend to leak, and add to drag. Bore caps on dry snorkels add to drag and complexity.

Very wide bore snorkels are difficult to clear, add to drag, and unduly increase "dead air space". Dead air space is the area in the breathing passage not exchanged with fresh air, but re-inhaled on the next breath. A snorkel with an over-sized bore or long length increases the volume of un-exhaled air.

Snorkels should have a smooth inner passageway. Avoid snorkels with corrugated internal bends. These tend to restrict clearing. Flex snorkels are popular and work well as long as they do not have internal ridges.

A medium bore, roughly 3/4 inch, snorkel with a tube long enough to extend above the surface when on the surface and looking straight down works well for most divers. With practice they can be used very efficiently. Of course, if you are more comfortable with a purge valve or dry snorkel, use it!

As taught in basic scuba classes, wearing the snorkel on the left side places the mouthpiece for the snorkel on one side and the regulator's mouthpiece on the other. This helps avoid confusing the snorkel mouth piece with the second stage regulator mouth piece. However for spearfishing, consider instead wearing the snorkel on the right side, where the second stage hose comes over your shoulder. Wearing it on the right side puts all of the gear that can tangle or interfere with head motion on the same side. You do not have to worry about the hoses on one side and the snorkel on the other. Everything is on the right side. As long as you can tell the difference between your snorkel and your regulator, it does not present a safety issue. On some snorkels the tube or mouthpiece angles slightly back, requiring that they be worn on the left side. This removes the option of wearing it on either side.

The side on which you wear your snorkel while scuba diving does not matter. Just make sure that you wear it on your mask where it is readily accessible upon surfacing. Some divers carry their snorkel in a bcd pocket or attached to a clip. This can create an awkward and perhaps dangerous situation on the surface with both hands holding spearfishing equipment and fish.

Buoyancy Compensating Device (bcd)

You see "personal preference" often in this book because most dive gear on the market today exhibits good quality and design. Most dive gear will work for spearfishing. Buoyancy compensators certainly represent a personal preference item; however, some features to look for in a bcd include:

- Comfortable fit;
- Bladder-less construction to reduce bulkiness and minimize trapped air;
- Shoulder releases to simplify removal;
- Large pockets with positive closures for storing extra equipment;
- "D" rings for attaching extra gear;
- Dependable inflation and deflation system with easy low pressure hose disconnect;
- Adjustable for wearing with or without an exposure suit.

One editorial comment; bcd inflator use and maintenance receives less attention than it deserves. You need to develop a high comfort level with using your bcd's inflator and dump valves. Small adjustments to the air volume in your bcd usually hold your buoyancy in balance. However, should you find yourself ascending unexpectedly, dump all of the air from your bcd then slowly re-establish proper buoyancy.

While it rarely occurs, inflator mechanisms occasionally stick in the open position and leak air into the bcd. A rapidly leaking inflator can result in an uncontrolled ascent. Even when diving within the no-decompression limits, surfacing faster than 60 feet per minute creates a dangerous situation. Making a three minute safety stop with a free flowing inflator mechanism is challenging.

What should you do when experiencing an uncontrolled ascent? A technique called "flaring", which involves coming up with your arms and legs spread while simultaneously dumping air through your bcd's purge valve, represents the most often recommended technique. However, another option involves disconnecting the inflator hose and then using manual inflation to control your buoyancy.

Prepare for this emergency by practicing disconnecting the inflator hose while the tank valve is open. It is a little more difficult to disconnect than with the pressure relieved from the low pressure hoses. Since you can not turn off your air, use both hands, with gloves on, to disconnect the hose.

You need to be as skilled in disconnecting the inflator hose as with picking up a dropped regulator. In addition, the inflator valve on the bcd and the inflator disconnect on the hose deserve servicing on the same maintenance schedule as your regulator. Servicing the inflator valve reduces the chance of it sticking. Servicing the disconnect ensures its smooth operation in the event that it needs disconnecting. Also, practice manually inflating your bcd. Always prepare for the worst; hope for the best!

Regulator

Other books contain entire chapters about regulators. As for regulator quality, manufacturers can not afford to build dangerous regulators. This is not to say that there are no bad regulators available; but, the well known manufacturers produce popular, proven models that provide years of reliable service. Many dive centers will let you rent a regulator then apply the rental cost to the purchase price if you buy from them. Here are a few of the features to consider when shopping for a regulator:

- Must breathe easily and drily in all attitudes and under various conditions, e.g., when you are horizontal, upside down, on your back, on either side, upright, and swimming vigorously.

- Reputable, available service (Some older, used regulators or uncommon brands are not easily serviced);
- At least 3 low and 1 high pressure port on the first stage;
- Good first stage manifold design with hoses arranged sensibly;
- The fewer the number of swivels and "O" rings the better;

Comments about second stages: Many manufacturers have developed "light weight, low profile" second stage regulators. Lower weight and less drag reduce jaw fatigue. Reducing jaw fatigue provides an excellent benefit as long as it avoids a sacrifice in functionality. Some of the early models of such regulators have weak second stage housings that crack after extended use. You may have seen recalls on this problem in some of the dive magazines. Reputable manufacturers stand behind their mistakes and correct defects but look for a model without weakness problems.

Another, more subtle design problem with some light weight, low profile second stages results from the exhaust ports being positioned farther forward than on older models. This presents no problem when a diver is looking primarily down or slightly ahead, but when looking out horizontally, exhaust bubbles flow in front of the face mask. For a spearfisherman this gives the fish an opportunity to slip away during the fog of bubbles. Evaluate the regulator before buying and talk to experienced spearfishermen.

Cylinders

Some scuba cylinders, which are popularly referred to as tanks, are made from steel alloys, others from aluminum. The popular aluminum "80's" hold approximately 80 cubic feet when filled to their maximum allowable pressure of 3000 psi. The actual volume varies depending upon cylinder manufacturer. Aluminum 80's provide adequate air for most diving. Divers who tend to use more air go with larger volume cylinders such as 90s, 100s, 120s, or some combination of doubles. Smaller divers who typically use less air sometimes prefer 65s or 50s. Larger cylinders and "doubles" provide more air but prove more difficult to maneuver and weigh more. For general recreational diving within the no decompression limits an 80, with a current hydrostatic test and recent visual inspection, meets most spearfishing demands. See PADI's *Encyclopedia of Diving* for additional information about tanks.

Weight belt

In diving you have uppers and you have downers..... Not those kinds of uppers and downers! The ones that increase or decrease buoyancy. Uppers include equipment such as bcd's, wetsuits, and natural body buoyancy. Downers primarily refer to weighting systems. Weights can be integral into the bcd or worn on a belt. A belt consists of either a traditional strap with hard weights threaded onto it, or a pouch belt with zipper or Velcro® closure pouches that accommodate either hard or soft weights.

When selecting a weighting system, consider the following points:

Weight integrated bcd

With weight integrated bcds, weights combine neatly with the tank and regulator within the bcd to form one unit. This simplifies gearing up by eliminating the need to wear a separate weight belt. A drawback to most weight integrated bcds becomes evident when boarding a boat. Weights can not be removed easily in the water. If the diver removes the bcd and tank before boarding the boat, someone must lift it into the boat. Lifting a weight integrated bcd into a boat poses a strenuous task.

Weight integrated bcd's should have quick releases to allow "dumping" the weights in case of emergency but operation of most quick releases results in the weights falling to the bottom. Some manufacturers offer bcds which provide the diver with a strap by which to maintain a grip on the weights after pulling them from the bcd. These bcds allow the diver to remove and hand aboard, some but not necessarily all, of the integrated weights before boarding the boat.

You should always familiarize yourself with the location and function of your dive buddy's weight releases. The importance of this increases with weight integrated bcds. Due to the variety of release designs, no standard quick release location or release function exists on weight integrated bcds.

Strap and hard weights

The traditional weight belt consists of a web belt with hard weights threaded onto it. It usually employs a flat, plastic, or stainless steel quick release buckle commonly found on bcds and weightbelts. Some older weight belts utilize a wire bale buckle. Pouches, that can be threaded onto the belt provide pouch belt benefits with a web belt. Strap belts can be removed separately and handed aboard to reduce weight when boarding the dive platform. Soft weights with straps sewn to them offer another strap belt option. Strap belts typically use hard, exposed weights which can damage equipment and toes if dropped. An advantage of strap belts lies in the ability to arrange weights independently for balance and comfort.

Pouch belts

Like strap belts, pouch belts use flat quick release buckles, allowing separate removal. Individual pouches can hold either hard or soft weights. Hard weights tend to wear out the pouch corners where the weights rub against the mesh. Adding or removing weights while in the water proves easier with pouch belts than with strap belts. Pouch belts provide the added benefit of allowing additional storage in unused pouches.

Personal preference governs the type of weighting system you use. Since it is especially important to swim level for energy conservation and stealth while spearfishing, some divers, whose legs tend to float, use ankle weights. Wearing the tank lower in the bcd or the primary weight belt lower around the waist provides an alternate technique for dealing with buoyant legs.

As you establish your optimum weighting requirements with different types and sizes of cylinders, exposure suits, and under various conditions, write them down in your log book for reference. In spearfishing, appropriate buoyancy is very important. A spearfisherman needs to move stealthily. Poorly balanced buoyancy makes this difficult.

Miscellaneous Dive Gear

OK, we've touched on the big items, now for the accessories. A spearfisherman should have:

- Gloves for hand protection. Garden gloves will work but dive gloves dry better and allow better dexterity;
- A small dive light attached by a lanyard and tucked away in a bcd pocket for use in looking under dark ledges;

- A sharp knife in a position where it can be removed with either hand. (Some spearfishermen attach it with electrical tie wraps or with Velcro® straps to the bcd's manual inflator hose. When doing this, avoid interfering with the inflator hose's action.);
- A small marker buoy and weight, coiled up and tucked away in a bcd pocket, for use in marking a spot to return to;
- A tucked away mesh bag for collecting trash or an unexpected lobster.

Summary

Most basic dive gear will serve the purpose for spearfishing. Look for name-brand dive gear that creates minimal drag and is easy to use.

Usually, equipment or equipment features that make diving easier will help when spearfishing. When you take up spearfishing, stay with the dive gear you already own until you recognize a compelling reason for purchasing something different.

The actual spearfishing sections of this book present additional gear considerations.... Read on!

Review Questions:
1. What is the overall consideration in the basic gear you chose to use while spearfishing?
2. Name three features to look for in choosing a mask for use in spearfishing.
3. How does a black skirt or color that prevents light from entering from the sides help underwater vision?
4. T/F Large, stiff bladed fins are best for divers with strong legs?
5. How are strap fins modified to prevent the straps from slipping or becoming entangled?
6. What is the purpose in selecting a snorkel without a "dry" feature?
7. How does a snorkel contribute to "dead air space"?
8. Why might it be advantageous to wear your snorkel on your right side instead of the accepted left side?
9. Why should the snorkel be worn on the mask, and not carried in a bcd pocket or clip?
10. List six considerations in choosing a bcd for use in spearfishing.
11. List five features to look for in a regulator used for spearfishing.
12. What is the most popular size of scuba cylinder and from what material are they made?
13. List the three types of primary weighting systems.
14. List five pieces of miscellaneous gear useful in spearfishing.

Chapter 3: Spearguns

Introduction

"'Bout time you got into the spearfishing stuff!"

Spearing fish sets spearfishing apart from other diving specialties. To spearfish, a diver needs to propel a spear with enough force and accuracy to penetrate a usually elusive fish. While muscle powered hand spears were once used, most divers now use a powered spear delivery system. Powered spear delivery systems include Hawaiian slings, pole spears, and mechanical spearguns. Surgical tubing powers most spear delivery systems. Pneumatic guns also enjoy popularity. Less prevalent power methods include compressed gas and spring power.

This chapter focuses on mechanical spearguns. Mechanical spearguns utilize a mechanical shaft catch and trigger release mechanism. **Chapter 4: Hawaiian Slings and Pole Spears** covers non-mechanical spear delivery devices.

Objectives - By the end of this section you should be able to:
1. Name the major speargun components.
2. List the types of spearshaft propulsion methods.
3. Identify the popular gun configurations and list their application.
4. Define the term "caught in the bight" and explain how to avoid becoming tangled in a speargun's line.
5. List the various types of line material used on line guns.

Basic speargun operation

"So, how does a speargun work?" Before it can be fired a gun must be loaded then cocked. Always do this with the safety on. Loading simply involves placing the spearshaft into the gun so that it locks firmly in the spearshaft catch mechanism. With band powered guns cocking consists of pulling each band back so that the wishbone catches in the spearshaft's band catch notch. (Wishbones are the thin solid wire, wire cable, monofilament, or nylon components of a band.) The single act of pressing the spearshaft into the gun's barrel simultaneously loads and cocks pneumatic guns.

Never cock or un-cock a speargun out of the water. Always do this while submerged. The lubrication provided by water reduces friction and wear during the cocking process. Firing a speargun out of water creates a safety hazard. See **Chapter 7: Speargun Safety** for additional speargun safety information.

To shoot a speargun, switch the safety to the "fire" position, sight down the barrel, and squeeze the trigger. Hold the gun butt away from your face to prevent injury from the gun's recoil. Always know your target and what lays behind it before pulling the trigger.

The above describes the basic concept of speargun operation. Gun operation varies depending upon gun type. Important speargun characteristics which affect operation include; gun length, power method, construction material, and configuration. The following discussion addresses the characteristics of various mechanical speargun types.

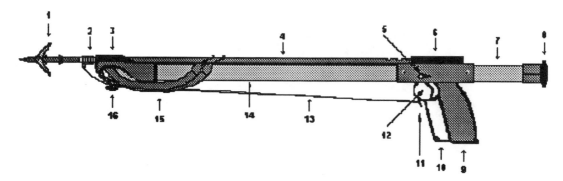

Figure 3-1 - Speargun Components.

1. Speartip
2. Line slide
3. Muzzle
4. Spearshaft
5. Safety
6. Shaft catch housing
7. Cocking stock or extension
8. Cocking plate or cocking butt
9. Handle housing
10. Knuckle guard
11. Line release
12. Trigger
13. Line
14. Barrel
15. Power bands
16. Line holder or keeper

Divers tend to refer to guns by names based upon their various characteristics. You've probably heard people refer to the same automobile as a luxury car, sports car, two door coup, high performance automobile, or red car, depending upon the point that they are making. Spearguns suffer the same confusing type of labeling. For example, the same gun may be called a long gun, wood gun, band gun, or line gun. You'll probably never hear a gun referred to as a long, wooden, band powered line gun.

Gun Length

Barrel length determines the effective length of a speargun. The measurement from the shaft catch mechanism to the end of the muzzle determines barrel length. Gun length is sometimes classified depending upon the length of spearshaft used. A properly sized shaft extends about 6 inches beyond the gun's muzzle.

Guns come in various lengths. Whether a gun receives classification as short or long depends upon subjective, relative judgment. For reference the table at the right suggests four size classifications.

Classification	Barrel
Short	18"-24"
Medium	25"-36"
Long	37"-54"
Extra-long	55"+

Long guns use shafts of approximately 42-60 inches. They provide superior range and accuracy. However, long guns require more effort to "sweep" through the water when lining up a shot on (tracking) a moving fish than short guns.

Short guns use shafts in the 24 inch range. They provide less range but offer more maneuverability, cock easier, and sweep through the water with less resistance than longer guns. The shortest guns are sometimes referred to as rock guns. They work best for short shots around rock piles and ledges. Some spearfishermen own a short gun in addition to their long gun(s).

Medium length guns use shafts of approximately 34-38 inches. They represent a compromise between the extended range and accuracy of long guns and the maneuverability of short guns. Divers who want an easily carried gun with which to spear an occasional fish may prefer medium length guns.

Blue water hunters, those who regularly target big, fast moving, deep water fish, such as tuna and wahoo, want a gun with long range, high velocity, and hard hitting power. Extra long guns meet this demand. Extra long guns, ones with barrels over 54 inches, are commonly used for taking big, usually pelagic fish, or in situations requiring long-range shots. The length of these guns makes loading and cocking difficult, requiring a long reach. Multiple, longer bands help make cocking them easier. For exciting reading about blue water hunting refer to *The Last of the Blue Water Hunters* by Carlos Eyles and *Blue Water Hunting* by Terry Maas.

Recommendation: Most spearfishermen target medium sized (five to fifteen pounds) fish in moderately clear, open water. Under these conditions a popular length, all around gun sports a 48 to 54 inch barrel and uses a 54 to 60 inch spearshaft. This length provides the range and accuracy to target larger fish and it can be used in tight quarters when positioned carefully.

Power Method

Most spearguns in use today utilize surgical tubing for power and are referred to as either band or sling guns. The next most common propulsion is pneumatic. Use of compressed gass and spring powered guns is rare.

Surgical tubing

A gun powered by surgical tubing corresponds as the underwater equivalent to a crossbow. Surgical tubing power bands consist of a hollow section of surgical tubing and a wishbone. Surgical tubing consist of latex rubber and comes in various colors, usually amber or black. Wishbones are the thin metal, monofilament, or nylon band component that fits into a spearshaft's band catch notch. Band length and diameter should match the speargun and suit an individual diver's strength and reach. A weak band will result in missed shots or in the shaft bouncing off of fish. An overly strong band will require extra effort to cock and cause inaccuracy.

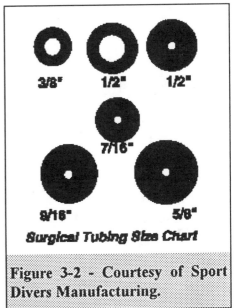

Figure 3-2 - Courtesy of Sport Divers Manufacturing.

The length of the surgical tubing of a power band determines its size. Band lengths commonly range from 9" to 30". Figure 3-2 shows cross-sections of common band material diameters. The hollow center of surgical tubing usually measures 1/8 inch. Larger inside diameter tubing with thinner wall is used on pole spears and Hawaiian slings. Some guns use multiple bands to allow easier cocking, while providing the necessary power. Others utilize a single, but relatively thick, strong band to reduce reloading and cocking time.

Pneumatic

With pneumatic spearguns, a sealed piston in the barrel propels the spearshaft. A pressurized air chamber inside of the speargun provides driving force to the piston. The air chamber is pressurized prior to diving by use of a hand pump, which is similar to a hand bicycle tire pump.

No air escapes from the chamber upon discharge so there is no need to surface and re-pump the pressure chamber. To cock the gun the spearfisherman uses a "T" handle to grip the spearpoint and press the spearshaft into the barrel. This pushes the piston down the barrel until it locks into the trigger mechanism. The single act of loading a pneumatic gun also cocks it.

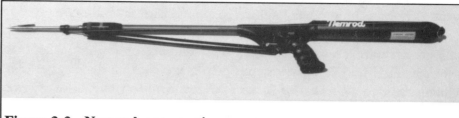

Figure 3-3 - Nemrod pneumatic speargun.

Figure 3-4 - SeaBear pneumatic speargun.

Pneumatic guns exhibit a high loading effort to spearshaft speed ratio. This means that, compared to a comparable single-band powered speargun, they are easier to cock with faster spearshaft speed.

Pneumatic guns require a "T" shaped handle to protect the diver's hand when cocking. Cocking handles come with the purchase of pneumatic guns. They may also be easily constructed from a piece of 4" x 3/4" PVC pipe with a speartip retainer hole drilled through one wall of the pipe near its center.

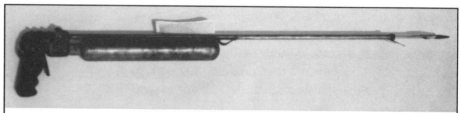

Figure 3-5 - Gawenis compressed gas gun, manufactured by Aerosonic Corporation, circa 1958. This gun used a 1800 psi compressed air cylinder to propel an O-ring fitted spearshaft. Unlike today's pneumatic guns, this gun released a blast of bubbles when discharged.

Some pneumatic guns come with interchangeable spearshafts and barrels This allows adjusting the gun's length to match expected spearfishing conditions.

On pneumatically, compressed gas, and spring powered guns, the muzzle, barrel, and handle comprise an integral unit. This integral unit houses the spearshaft guide, propulsion, and trigger mechanisms. Otherwise, the basic components and the technique for hunting with the differently powered guns are similar.

Which power method is best? Personal preference dictates which power method you select. Band powered guns offer simplicity and reliability. Their components are readily available and they are versatile. Many spearfishing tournament winners use band powered guns; however, some champion spearfishermen prefer pneumatically powered guns. Pneumatic guns possess several attributes. The process of loading and cocking pneumatic guns consists of one motion. Pneumatic guns are lightweight, easily maneuvered, and hold a reputation for high accuracy and spearshaft speed. The internal piston, which propels the shaft from a pneumatic gun, provides power to the shaft for the full length of the barrel. With band powered guns the propelling force stops once the band returns to its un-cocked length. As for drawbacks, with their various

"O" ring and other seals, some divers consider pneumatic guns more difficult to maintain than band powered guns.

As previously mentioned, compressed gas, and spring powered guns enjoy limited use. Guns powered by compressed gas expel a blast of bubbles underwater. The bubbles temporarily hinder the spearfisherman's vision and frighten the fish.

Construction Material

Common construction materials used in spearguns include plastic, aluminum, stainless steel, and wood. Stainless steel comprises most mechanical parts. The main distinguishing component of a gun is the barrel. It is either made of aluminum, stainless tubing, or wood. Just as guns are sometimes referred to by their power method, they are sometimes called metal or wood guns, depending upon their barrel construction material. This applies mainly to band powered guns, since pneumatic and spring powered guns are constructed of metal tubing. Handles and muzzles can be constructed of plastic or metal.

"Which is best, metal or wood?" "Personal preference" comes into play again with your choice. The following section presents the characteristics of each construction material. You will find divers who swear by each type.

Figure 3-6 - Stainless tubing barreled AB Biller Sea Hornet speargun. Note individual nylon shaft guides placed at regular intervals. Photograph courtesy of AB Biller Company.

Metal gun

The stainless or aluminum tubing used in metal speargun muzzles consists of hollow, round or rectangular extrusions. It contains internal seals to prevent water from filling the hollow space. The internal air space created by the seals

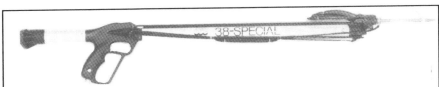

Figure 3-7 - Speargun with aluminum barrel. This gun has a plastic shaft guide under the spearshaft. This serves to improve accuracy and reduce noise. Photograph courtesy of JBL Enterprises, Inc.

provides buoyancy. With spearshaft unloaded some metal guns float. Plastic guides, attached to the top of the barrel, serve to channel the spearshaft in a straight trajectory and dampen the sound of the gun's discharge. Metal guns offer a more slender profile than wooden guns. This reduces resistance when "tracking" a moving fish. Drilling holes in the tubing for the attachment of accessories, such as spare spearshaft holders, line reels, and line clips, invites breakdown in the tubing's water tight integrity and accelerates corrosion.

Wood Gun

As a barrel material, wood, either varnished mahogany or oiled teak, provides natural flotation. Drilling pilot holes in

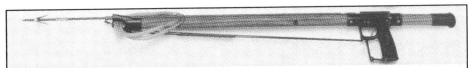

Figure 3-8 - Wood (teak) "Sea Hornet" speargun. Courtesy of AB Biller Company.

the wood allows attachment of accessories with screws or bolts. A shaft guide groove, milled directly into the top surface of the wooden barrel, helps the spearshaft track straight and wood acts as a natural sound dampener. A wood gun's wider muzzle profile creates more drag when sighting and "tracking" a fish than that of a metal barreled gun.

Gun Configurations

There are five basic speargun configurations which this book classifies as: 1) Freeshaft; 2) Line; 3) Combination; 4) Double-barreled; and, 5) Hybrid. Freeshaft guns and line guns are fundamental gun configurations. Other gun

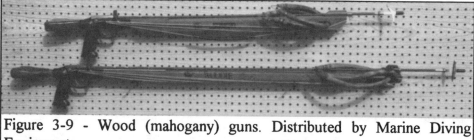

Figure 3-9 - Wood (mahogany) guns. Distributed by Marine Diving Equipment.

types represent variations of these two types. With a freeshaft gun the spearshaft is unencumbered. It does not have an attached line. On a line gun the spearshaft has a line attached to it. The line usually attaches to the muzzle of the gun but can be attached to a reel mounted on the gun or a surface buoy. A combination gun includes a spare spearshaft holder which holds either an extra freeshaft or lineshaft. If one of the spearshafts is a lineshaft, the spearfisherman switches between the two spearshafts, depending upon his anticipated quarry. A double-barreled gun mimics a double-barreled shotgun or over and under firearm. It's configuration varies with different combinations of line and freeshafts. A double-barreled gun differs from a combination gun in that it contains a dual loading capability with two independent trigger mechanisms. A hybrid gun resembles a freeshaft or combination gun except that the spearshaft has a low profile line slide and a speartip milled into the shaft.

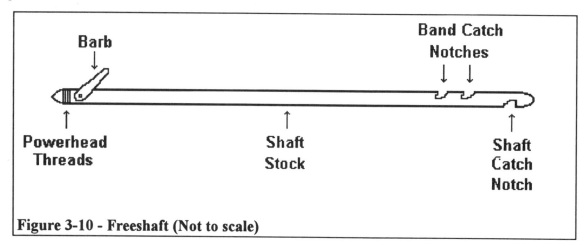

Figure 3-10 - Freeshaft (Not to scale)

In addition to the five basic configurations there are three special types of line gun. They include reel gun, float buoy gun, and butt wrapped line gun. The following section describes speargun configurations in more detail.

Freeshaft gun

Despite their apparent simplicity, freeshaft guns come in a variety of configurations. The distinguishing feature of a freeshaft gun is its unattached spearshaft. The primary advantage of using freeshafts lies in their speed, range and smoother release from the gun. These features improve long range accuracy. By contrast a typical lineshaft is slower, with less range, and provides less long range accuracy. Removing the line from the spearshaft of a lineshaft gun technically converts it to a freeshaft gun. The spearshaft would be faster and have a longer range without the drag of the line to slow it down. However, a freeshaft gun is more than a line gun with the line removed.

By design freeshafts differ from lineshafts. Lineshafts typically carry a screw on speartip, a line slide, and a slide stop. The typical screw on speartip used on a lineshaft includes two or more barbs and a barb hold down ring, which aids in removing fish.

A freeshaft contains a point milled directly into the end of the spearshaft itself. Freeshafts usually carry a single hinged barb attached directly to the spearshaft. Freeshafts do not require a barb hold down ring. To remove fish simply slide them completely off the back end of the spearshaft. Both freeshafts and lineshafts provide band catch notches (band powered guns only) and shaft catch surfaces. These are milled into the spearshaft.

As a result of the built-in speartip and lack of a line slide, freeshafts weigh less for given length, exhibit better balance, and create less resistance than a lineshaft. These factors contribute to provide faster shaft speed, longer range, and better accuracy.

Freeshafts reduce fish tear-offs. Without the resistance of an attached line, a freeshaft tends to stay implanted in the fish rather than tearing free. Since they do not need to stand up to the leverage of a line pulling against the spearshaft, some freeshafts come in a smaller diameter than lineshafts. A smaller diameter increases spearshaft speed by further reducing weight.

Figure 3-11 - Nice grouper.

"Don't fish swim off with the spearshaft?" It can happen but freeshafts are typically used with fish under fifteen pounds or with fish that tend to "hole up" after being shot. In addition, the improved accuracy and speed provided by a freeshaft results in more frequent "kill" or "stone" shots. Highly successful spearfishermen know where to stone the fish they hunt. However, even a relatively small fish, hit in a non-vital area can swim off with a spearshaft. Accuracy is important.

Freeshaft guns come in a variety of barrel lengths. They typically range between 48 to 60 inches. The most common freeshaft measures approximately 60 inches. A 60 inch shaft works well in a 48" gun even though the shaft protrudes excessively from the end of the gun. The extra length of the spearshaft offsets the additional weight by providing a smoother trajectory. Since guns shorter than about 48 inches are typically used when range and speed are less important, they are usually not rigged as freeshaft guns.

Powering freeshafts with one strong band improves efficiency. Having only one band to cock and no line to re-wrap reduces reload time. Most spearguns can carry multiple bands. With only one band required to power the spearshaft additional bands become spares. When using a single, strong band, avoid making the band too strong. You should not need to strain to cock it. Too strong of a band adversely affects accuracy. Also, overpowering a freeshaft will result in the shaft passing completely through small fish.

Line gun
Line guns provide the advantage of maintaining a connection between the underwater hunter and his prey. Line guns work well around wrecks, around ledges with deep undercuts, and in limited visibility situations. The line allows for easier retrieval of a spearshaft and limits the range of the spearshaft for added safety.

Though line gun configurations vary widely, the typical rig consists of a gun with a line attached between its muzzle and a spearshaft line slide. The line usually extends two or four times the gun's length. A mechanical line keeper holds the line in place and releases the line when the trigger is pulled. As described in the section on freeshafts, lineshafts typically carry a screw on speartip; a line slide, and have a slide stop knurled into the spearshaft. (Refer the Kevlar line discussion later in this chapter for a non-slide ring variation.)

A typical screw-on speartip for a line gun carries one or more hinged barbs and a barb hold down ring. The hold down ring aids in fish removal. Some configurations, particularly

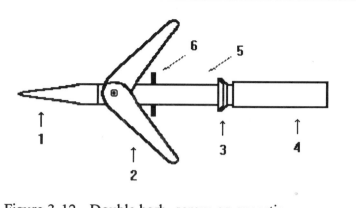

Figure 3-12 - Double barb, screw-on speartip.

1. Spearpoint   4. Threaded collar
2. Double hinged barbs   5. Shaft stock
3. Barb hold down   6. Barb springs
                                    (rubber)

those used for large fish, include a detachable or "slip" tip. A special barbless speartip provides a safety feature with large fish. A barbless speartip allows the diver to pull the spearshaft out of a fish which has been hit in a non-vital spot. Refer to **Chapter 6: Technique** and **Chapter 5: Special Equipment** for information on speartip options and their application.

Lineshafts, since they need to stand up to the leverage of a line pulling against them, sometimes have a thicker diameter than freeshafts. Lineshafts, like freeshafts, have band catch notches (band powered guns only) and shaft catch surfaces milled into them. They also include a slide ring stop milled into them. This keeps the line slide from sliding off the end of the spearshaft.

Beginners often choose line guns because they offer the convenience and added safety of keeping the spear attached to the gun. However, line guns demand special safety precautions.

The line or cable connecting the spearshaft to the gun or surface float can itself present a danger. A fighting fish can entangle and "wrap up" a careless spearfisherman. In seafaring, a standard warning is; "Don't stand in the bight!" This means, Do not stand or place any part of your body inside of a loop (bight) which forms in a line. Should the line suddenly become tight it can trap you in the loop. This warning applies with any line such as fishing line, docking line, and, in this instance, to a line connected between a diver and a fighting fish.

Proper positioning and technique can reduce this danger when spearfishing with a line gun:

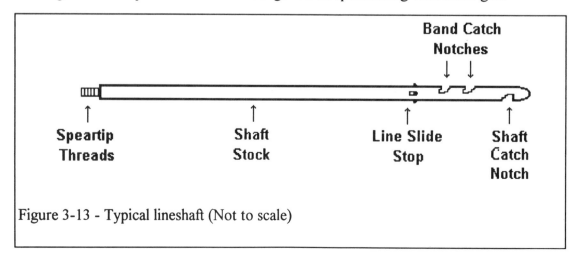

Figure 3-13 - Typical lineshaft (Not to scale)

- Avoid spearfishing with a line gun near an anchor line, suspended cables, oil platforms, or other obstructions. Once a fish bends a line around an obstruction it tends to continue circling the obstruction and wrapping the line around the obstruction. A diver caught inside of the circle can become pinned and literally tied to the obstruction.
- On hookah rigs the air hose provides a built in obstruction around which line can tangle. Avoid spearfishing while using a hookah rig or limit your quarry to small fish which can not swim with the spearshaft.
- Always face a speared fish by turning your body to follow it during its fight and allow nothing between you and the fish.
- Use a shooting line no longer than the effective range of your gun. Longer lines reduce your control over the line and increase the danger of entanglement.
- Prevent small loops, which can entangle arms, legs, fingers, equipment, etceteras, from forming in the line. Never deliberately wrap a line around your hand to improve your grip. You may find that the line has you rather than you having it.
- While diving or topside, practice staying out of the bight when handling any line. Take particular care when retrieving toss buoys. While you are winding the line around a buoy the weight sometimes hangs on the bottom. Pulling on the buoy to force the weight from the bottom sometimes results in the line jumping off the end of the buoy. When this happens it can easily wrap around your hand or a finger. Even a small line under strain from the inertia of a boat can cause severe injury.

Figure 3-14 - Caught in bight. Courtesy of Wayne Butts.

Don't get wrapped up in your sport. Stay out of the bight!

Being towed by a large fish can also create a risky situation. You must be willing to let go of your gun in the event that a large fish tows you dangerously. The word "dangerously" covers various situations. They include being towed:

- Deeper than is safe;
- Into an overhead environment;
- For a longer period of time than planned for the dive;
- Around an obstruction;
- Up faster than a safe ascent rate.

You should also release the gun and fish if vital dive equipment, such as mask or regulator, becomes displaced or malfunctions. After correcting your equipment problem you can usually relocate the fish, follow it safely, and retrieve it along with your gun.

The above describes popular line gun configurations and special line gun safety precautions. However, many considerations enter into configuring a line gun. These include: gun length, line material, line attachment options, and other special gun configurations. The following describes various line gun features and options. The first topic addresses the line materials and how they are used.

Nylon and Dacron®
Line material includes braided nylon, Kevlar, Dacron, stainless steel, shock cord, monofilament, and "slinky" cord line materials. Braided nylon enjoys the most popularity but understanding the features of other materials will help in choosing line material. *Note: Dacron is a registered tradename of the Dupont Chemical Corporation.*

Braided nylon exhibits good knot holding ability, resists abrasion and breakdown from sunlight, flexes freely, and provides a slight amount of shock absorbing stretch. Dacron offers marginally better knot holding ability and provides about the same abrasion and breakdown resistance as nylon, but stretches less. A fairly small diameter, 1/8 to 3/16 inch, nylon or Dacron line works well for line gun material. The smaller the line, the less drag it adds to the spearshaft; however, thin line gives way to abrasion more easily.

A bowline provides a good knot for attaching nylon and Dacron line to the spearshaft and gun. A shock cord or surgical tubing "shock absorber" tied in-line with nylon or Dacron serves three purposes: 1) Provides elastic "slack" when wrapping the line between the muzzle and the line keeper; 2) Dampens the jolt of the spearshaft hitting the end of the line, reducing wear and line slide jams; 3) Reduces fish tear-offs by absorbing some of the strain of the fight.

Polypropylene
Polypropylene, another synthetic material, does not work as well as other line gun materials due to three properties; 1) It holds knots poorly; 2) It breaks down easily in sunlight; and, 3) It tends to "expand" due to the springy nature of its fibers to a relatively larger diameter than other materials. However, because it floats it makes excellent "trailer" or "backing" line when used in a float buoy line gun configuration. (See the discussion on float buoy line guns later in this chapter for additional information.)

Steel Cable
Stainless steel cable represents the strongest material used for spearfishing line. It is relatively stiff, must be secured to the spearshaft and to the gun with cable crimps or wire splices, exhibits effectively no stretch, and strongly resists abrasion. Stainless cable enjoys popularity when spearing large pelagic fish. Since it possesses great strength, a relatively small, 1/8 inch or so, diameter cable can be used. As with nylon and Dacron, a shock absorber sometimes attaches in-line with stainless cable.

One safety consideration with cable: Because it resists abrasion so effectively, cutting stainless cable can prove very difficult, almost impossible, in case of emergency. This brings particular concern since rigs targeting large fish often employ stainless cable. Spearfishermen have been known to become "wrapped up" in cable by large fish and unable to cut their way free. Inserting a weak link, such as a shock absorber, may help but the weak link may prove un-reachable in a problem situation. A small pair of wire cutters, carried in an easily accessible location, will help reduce risk of spearfishing with cable.

"Meat hooks" pose another hazard with stainless cable. As cable wears from use, individual strands of the cable break and protrude from the body of the cable. This creates small pin and needle burrs which can poke holes through the best of gloves and toughest of hands. Take special care with stainless steel cable.

Shock Cord
"Oh Boy, bungie fishing!" For super shock absorption a line composed completely of shock cord provides the most "give". Shock cord provides strength, exhibits less flexibility than nylon or Dacron, must be secured with crimps or wraps of small line, and tends to be of thicker diameter than other materials. However, divers who use it report shock cord greatly reduces fish loss due to tear-offs. Since it is typically used for large

pelagic fish at short range, the added resistance of its relatively larger diameter creates less concern for loss of shaft speed and range. Instead of two loops (four gun lengths), shock cord usually measures long enough for just one loop (two gun lengths).

Monofilament

Heavy gauge monofilament, the kind typically used for commercial longline fishing, represents the material of choice on some large fish rigs. Much the same

Figure 3-15 - Monofilament configuration muzzle. Note snap disconnect on low profile lineslide and custom muzzle assembly. This is a customized AB Biller Sea Hornet available from Spearfishing Specialties.

as stainless cable, monofilament exhibits high strength, stretches little, resists abrasion and rot, must be attached with cable style crimps, and is fairly stiff.

The typical monofilament rig differs from configurations that use other line materials. When attached to the gun, one or both ends of the line are fitted with a safety pin type clip or other strong snap clip. The clip allows quick attachment to the gun and spearshaft, providing convenient conversion between line and freeshaft configurations. The line measures only two gun lengths.

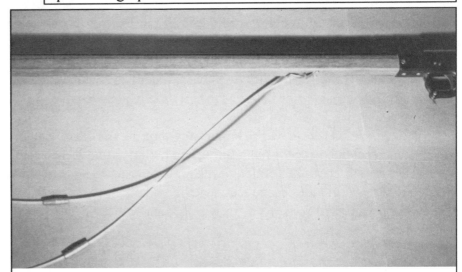

Figure 3-16 - Monofilament configuration showing use of under-barrel clip for holding line in shooting position instead of using the gun's mechanical line release.

Instead of using the gun's mechanical line keeper, a spring clip attached to the back, underside of the gun's barrel, holds the slack line in place. Two slide weights, one positioned on either side of the spring clip, hold the slack down and out of the way. No shock absorber, other than the resistance of the line and slide weights, is used on this line rig.

Monofilament offers one advantage over stainless cable. It develops no "meat hooks". Use it with the same warning as stainless cable and carry a small pair of wire cutters. It strongly resists cutting with a knife.

Auto Coil ®

Coiled monofilament (Auto Coil ®) speargun lines, sometimes called "slinky" cords, have become popular within the last few years. Coiled monofilament consists of much thinner material than that used on the monofilament rig described previously. Coil line flexes easily, comes fitted with swivels and key ring style attachment rings, exhibits a high degree of strength, and provides built in shock absorbency. Because the line coils up compactly it eliminates the need to place it in the line keeper. This speeds gun loading. Its drawbacks include a tendency for the coil to tangle in rock or dive gear. Coil lines work especially well on pneumatic and short "rock" guns.

Kevlar®

Kevlar, a relatively modern synthetic material, exhibits little stretch and approaches steel in strength. Line made from Kevlar works well on line guns in the same type of applications as either stainless steel wire rope or pre-stretched Dacron. It flexes more freely than wire rope and provides more strength than Dacron. *Note: Kevlar is a registered tradename of the Dupont Chemical Corporation.*

Some manufacturers make special spearshafts for use with Kevlar. These spearshafts have a line attachment hole drilled through the back end of the spearshaft. The Kevlar line passes through the hole, secured with a bowline knot. This eliminates the

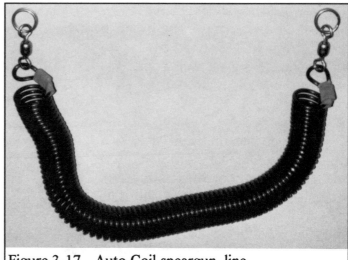

Figure 3-17 - Auto Coil speargun line.

bulky line slide. These spearshafts resemble freeshafts in their weight and construction. They have a built in speartip and no line slide stop. The spearshaft usually includes one or two oversized hinged barbs.

When loaded the line leads back through the muzzle and lies parallel to the spearshaft. It secures to the gun's mechanical line keeper or in a spring clip mounted under the barrel stock. When the gun is fired the line feeds out through the muzzle along with the spearshaft. Due to the reduced resistance and weight, this special spearshaft provides range and speed comparable to a freeshaft, along with the advantages of a line gun. A sharp knife and some types of wire cutters will cut Kevlar. Test your knife or cutters before relying upon either.

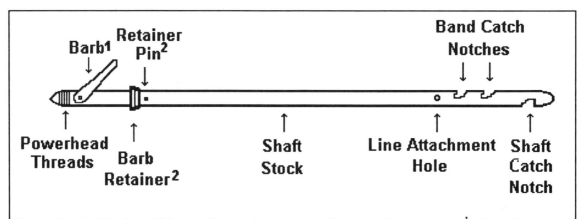

Figure 3-18 - Kevlar, slide-less lineshaft. Note the line attachment hole. [1] Oversized barb [2] Barb retainer & retainer pin optional.

Since there are no barb hold down rings on the built in speartip, removing a fish requires a special technique. Holding down the oversized barbs and backing the shaft out works for small fish. On larger fish passing the spearshaft completely through the fish then passing it back through point first eliminates the need for a barb hold down ring (retainer).

Line gun variations

Just as line comes in a variety of materials, line guns come in a variety of configurations. Reel gun, float buoy, and butt wrap line gun configurations provide for attaching a longer line to the spearshaft. A longer line helps in landing large fish or fish which run under ledges. A longer line demands more attention to avoid becoming wrapped up or entangled. The next several topics discuss line extending options provided by these configurations.

Reel gun

Attaching a reel to the back, underside of the barrel converts a line gun into a reel gun. The reel permits use of a much longer line. Line gun reels are stoutly constructed to withstand the strain of a fighting fish. Lightweight "cave diving" reels are unsuitable for use on spearguns. Either a standard lineshaft, usually with a detachable tip, or Kevlar style lineshaft works well in reel guns.

Wrapping the line once or twice between the end of the gun and the line release usually provides sufficient "shooting slack". The gun's mechanical line release may be unusable due to the interfering position of the reel. In this situation a spring clip, attached forward of the reel, holds the shooting slack.

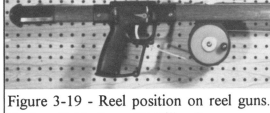

Figure 3-19 - Reel position on reel guns. Reel available from AB Biller Company.

Some manufacturers provide an adjustable drag on their reels for fighting fish. Reels without drags require that the diver use a gloved hand to press the line against the underside of the barrel for drag tension. A line guide attached to the underside of the muzzle keeps the line leading forward, parallel to the underside of the barrel.

Typical reel gun line measures approximately seventy feet but varies, depending upon water depth and size of fish being pursued. Deeper water or larger fish calls for longer line. Reel capacity and line thickness govern maximum line length.

Some reel guns employ two line materials, joined securely together. The first fifteen foot, "shooting slack" section of the line should be of a heavy, chafe resistant line material such as Dacron or Kevlar. "Backing" material, which makes up most of the line's length, can be a thinner line.

Figure 3-20 - Speargun reel. Courtesy Riffe International.

Monofilament, due to it's slippery nature, complicates controlling the line as it pays out from the reel. Monofilament also requires more careful handling. It is difficult to see, increasing the risk of entanglement.

(Refer to the discussion of Butt Wrapped line guns for a description of incorporating a CO_2 inflatable float to a reel gun.)

Float buoy and break-away rigs

Float buoy, also known as "Mexican" (Last of the Blue Water Hunters, pg. 139) or "breakaway" (Shark Hunters, pg. 17), rigs provide extended line length by tethering a line directly from a lineshaft to a surface float. A "gun tethered" float buoy rig works on the same principle but the buoy line is tied to the gun instead of to the spearshaft. Float buoy rigs allow freedivers to shoot relatively large fish then surface to "play" the fish. For fish that "hole up" under a ledge, freedivers use the float buoy line as a surface reference to guide them back to their quarry.

On a "breakaway" float buoy rig the spearshaft loads into the gun with the line feeding directly from the spearshaft to the surface float. A variation allows the use of "shooting slack". In the shooting slack configuration either the mechanical line release or a spring clip on the underside of the barrel holds the line in place, releasing it when the gun is fired.

One technique for attaching the line on a breakaway rig incorporates the use of a shooting

Figure 3-21 - Lifeguard torpedo buoy adapted for spearfishing use. Buoy is counter weighted to hold a flag upright. Available from Riffe International.

slack "leader". One end of the leader attaches to the spearshaft. The other end attaches to the float line and holds a small shock cord loop. The shock cord loop provides holding tension to keep the shooting slack hooked on the mechanical line release.

A "gun tethered" float buoy rig loads in the same general manner as a line gun. Instead of being attached to the spearshaft, the float attaches to the speargun. The float line allows the diver to release the gun, surface and "play" a large fish or orient on a fish which "holes up".

Figure 3-22 - Note special floating tubing used instead of line. This reduces tangles.

Buoys must be durable and provide adequate flotation. Boat fenders or large bullet shaped net floats make good buoys. Most divers who use float buoy rigs prefer as little drag as possible. A streamlined buoy reduces the effort needed to tow the float line and buoy.

Floating polypropylene line, the kind used for ski ropes, makes excellent float buoy line. Use a length about 1 1/2 to 2 times the expected water depth. To make the line length easily adjustable borrow a trick from water skiers. Prepare a main length with an eye splice in the buoy end. Prepare several extension pieces with eye splices in each end. The lines are attached to each other by looping them together. Adjust the float line's length by adding or removing extension sections.

Another length adjusting technique involves use of a grooved commercial fishing buoy. Wrap excess line into the notched section until the desired length remains. Use two half hitches to hold the line in place.

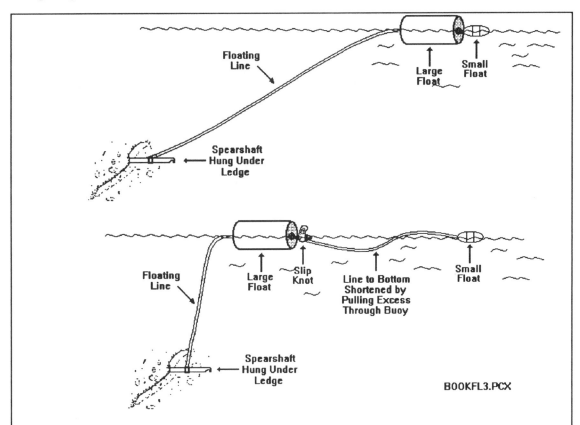

Figure 3-23 - Technique for shortening the distance between a freediver and a fish wedged under a ledge. During normal diving and swimming the line is left long to reduce drag. When a fish wedges under a ledge it is shortened to position the diver directly over the ledge.

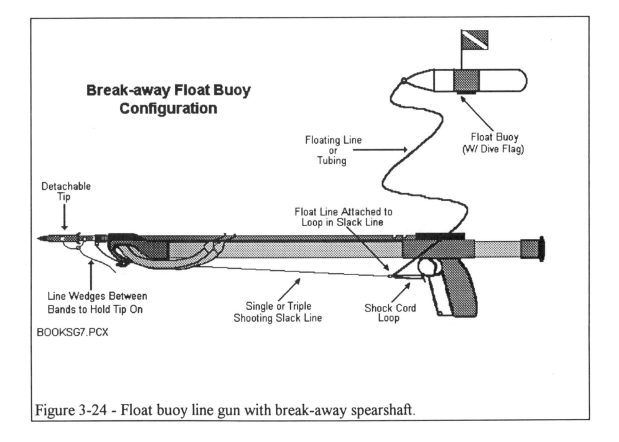

Figure 3-24 - Float buoy line gun with break-away spearshaft.

A trick, useful for freediving, employs a sliding buoy to adjust the line length for various water depths. Set this system up by using a buoy, such as a net float, with a small hole through its center. Run the float line through the hole and secure it with a smaller stopper buoy, stopper plate, or stopper knot. The stopper keeps the line from sliding completely out of the buoy. When a speared fish swims under a ledge or into a wreck, the freediver surfaces. He then shortens the line by sliding it through the buoy and holding it in place temporarily with a slip knot. This shortens the distance between diver and fish. After retrieving the fish, removing the slip knot allows the float to slide back to the end of the line. Remember to avoid becoming tangled in the line.

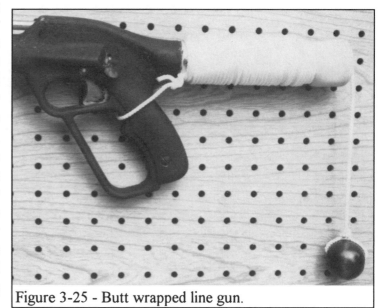

Figure 3-25 - Butt wrapped line gun.

Butt wrapped line gun

A butt wrap rig consists of a regular line gun with a separate length of 1/8 inch, or so, nylon line, approximately thirty feet long, wrapped around its cocking stock (butt). One end of the line attaches to the gun, the other is secured so that it will break free

Figure 3-26 - Butt wrapped line gun, "released".

Figure 3-27 - CO_2 float attached to stock of a reel gun. Top photo shows float rolled. A pull of the CO_2 lanyard and the float inflates as shown in bottom photo.

Figure 3-28 - CO_2 float attachment. Note hole through cocking stock and special line clip used to secure the float to the gun.

when pulled. This versatile configuration represents a modified version of the float line gun. It works like a float buoy rig except that the diver serves as the float. The cocking stock's length limits the amount of line to the length available in two wrapped layers.

Wrapping works best on an aluminum gun that uses a "chair leg" style rubber butt cap. Punch a hole in the end of the rubber cap. Lead one end of the line through the hole and knot it to hold it in place. Attach the other end of the line to the gun's handle. Then wrap it tightly around the butt. Secure the line by pressing the butt cap onto the end of the gun. The friction of the butt cap holds the line in place until a need to deploy the butt wrap arises. A strong rubber band, such as one cut from a bicycle inner tube, can be used on guns without rubber caps.

Tie a large stopper knot or thread a large, 3/4 to 1 inch, bead to the free end of the line. This provides a grip. Deploy the butt wrap by pulling off the butt cap, allowing the extra line to unwrap from the gun butt.

Some divers make a loop in the free end, but this is dangerous and not advised. A loop around your wrist or fingers can twist and close so tightly that you can not free yourself, creating a dangerous situation. Hans Haas in his book *Challenging the Deep* gives an exciting account of a close call he experienced when he tied himself to his spear then shot a large fish. He almost drown before he cut the line. (Also, see "Stay out of the bight!" earlier in this chapter for safety precautions when using line guns.)

Fitting a gun with a CO_2 inflatable float combines the concept of a butt wrapped rig or a reelgun with a float buoy rig. The inflatable float mounts to the cocking stock section of the gun. Discharging the float's CO_2 cartridge inflates it, providing a tether to the surface. Some divers attach the buoy directly to a standard line gun. They rely upon

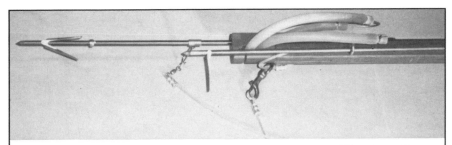

Figure 3-29 - Combination gun, muzzle end. AB Biller Sea Hornet with customizations available from Spearfishing Specialties.

the lift of the buoy to float the gun to the surface once the fish becomes exhausted.

On a butt wrapped line gun, be sure to completely test and practice with your particular configuration. The gun must be free to "wobble" as the line unwraps from the butt. A gun with a wide cocking plate for a butt cap or a gun stuck at an angle under a ledge may not unwrap freely. Experiment under controlled conditions until you are confident that your rig works effectively.

Combination gun

Combination guns provide various options for configuring your speargun. A spare shaft holder distinguishes a combination gun from other setups. A spare shaft holder consists of a milled stainless or brass loop mounted on the gun's forward section and a thumb screw or friction mount bolted to the back section. A spare spearshaft slides into the front mount and secures in the back mount. On screw mounts the screw should fit securely into one of the spearshaft's band catch notches to ensure a firm grip on the shaft. To make their own mount, some divers use a stainless eye bolt for the front mount and short length of rubber hose or friction shaft holder for the back mount.

A combination gun provides the option of carrying a line and a freeshaft or two freeshafts on your gun. Two lineshafts should not be used due to the danger of entanglement. When carrying a combination of free and lineshafts, load the most likely needed spearshaft into the gun. If a need for the other spearshaft arises during a dive, switch spearshafts by either discharging the gun or unloading the gun and reloading with the desired spearshaft. Keep an eye on your shaft to avoid losing it during the switching process.

When using a float buoy rig on a combination gun the breakaway configuration provides the most versatility. The breakaway allows the diver to reload the unattached gun with the spare freeshaft after shooting a fish with the float rigged lineshaft.

Standard line guns and guns with breakaway rigs represent two options for attaching a line to one of the spearshafts. However, spare spearshaft holders interfere with the function of a butt wrap configuration. For this reason, butt wrapped rigs can not be used as combination guns.

Double-barreled gun

Spearfishermen often report missing a shot at an elusive fish only to have it return within annoyingly easy range. Then, just as the diver completes reloading, the fish darts out of range. Some divers construct their own solution to this situation. They build double-barreled guns by bolting two guns together. A spacer separates the two barrels. Having two spearshafts cocked and ready to release gives the hunter a second shot when the fish doubles-back within range. These guns are bulky but if you're a bad shot....

In the past, Ultimate marketed a double-barreled speargun. Though no longer in production, these "factory made" double-barreled guns remain available on the used market. They employ separate trigger mechanisms and power bands for each spearshaft. Because both shafts load into the same muzzle and handle, these guns offer a more streamlined profile than that provided by bolting two guns together.

Use only one lineshaft on double-barreled guns. This reduces the possibility of becoming "hog tied" after shooting two separate fish.

Hybrid line gun

A hybrid line gun provides the advantage of being easily switched between line or freeshaft configurations. The hybrid gun's special spearshaft distinguishes it from either a line gun or freeshaft gun. This spearshaft resembles a freeshaft with a built in speartip. However, its low profile line slide includes an enlarged line attachment eye which simplifies converting the spearshaft to a lineshaft. A snap clip can be attached to the line slide for a line gun configuration. To quickly convert the shaft back to a freeshaft simply remove the clip. With the clip detached, the hybrid shaft's range

Figure 3-30 - Hybrid line gun. Note low-profile lineslide and quick connect clip. AB Biller Sea Hornet customized by Spearfishing Specialties.

approaches that of a freeshaft. A machined line stop or pin prevents the line slide from sliding off the end of the spearshaft.

Some divers add a barb hold down ring directly to the spearshaft to aid in fish removal when used in the lineshaft configuration. Other divers push the shaft all the way through the fish, turn it around, and then pass it point first back through the fish to remove the shaft.

To keep the line neatly stored when not attached to the spearshaft a loop at the muzzle serves to retain the clip. Cutting the line to just the right length allows it to wedge securely around the end of the cocking plate. When used as a line gun, a spring clip, mounted to the underside of the barrel, holds the line. The mechanical line release is not used.

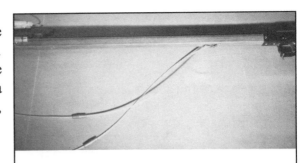

Figure 3-31 - Hybrid line gun. Note slide weights on line and spring clip on underside of barrel.

Summary

With the many options in length, power method, construction material, and configuration, which gun do you choose?

Spearguns represent a spearfisherman's tools. A carpenter chooses a claw hammer over a sledge hammer for driving a nail. Similarly, a spearfisherman needs to use the right speargun for a particular spearfishing situation. Though the various options of freeshaft, lineshaft, reel, and float buoy rigs provide a confusing array of configurations, keep it simple at first. Just as various courses provide a beginning scuba diver with a gradual path to becoming an expert diver, a spearfisherman should build up to more challenging forms of spearfishing and gun configurations. A high quality 48" to 54" barrel line gun makes a good all-around first gun. Practice with the line gun on small fish in shallow water and work up to larger game under more challenging conditions. After gaining experience with the lineshaft purchase a couple of freeshafts and work your way back up, beginning with small fish again.

After becoming comfortable using lineshafts and freeshafts, determine if you need a more elaborate configuration. When selecting a gun for a particular type of spearfishing, study various models used by experienced spearfishermen for that type of hunting. Other contemporary books on spearfishing include: *The Last of the Blue Water Hunters* by Carlos Eyles and *Blue Water Hunting* by Terry Maas.

Whichever gun you choose, insist upon high quality. This is not the piece of equipment upon which to save money! A high quality, well-maintained speargun will give many years of service.

Review Questions:

1. For each of the speargun components listed below, match the number from the diagram.

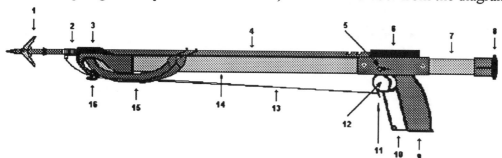

Speartip: _____
Line Slide: _____
Muzzle: _____
Spearshaft: _____
Safety: _____
Shaft lock mechanism housing: _____
Cocking stock: _____
Cocking plate or cocking butt: _____
Handle housing: _____
Knuckle guard: _____
Line release: _____
Trigger: _____
Line: _____
Barrel: _____
Power bands: _____
Line keeper: _____

2. T/F A longer gun and spearshaft generally provides longer range and accuracy than a shorter gun.
3. T/F A longer gun is easier to sweep through the water and is more maneuverable than a shorter gun.
4. T/F When a spear is loaded in a pneumatic gun, the gun is also cocked and ready to shoot.
5. T/F Guns are sometimes distinguished variously as wood or metal guns and as pneumatic or band powered guns.
6. T/F Freeshaft guns and line guns are the basic gun configurations.
7. Which gun type, freeshaft or line gun, typically has the most range, spearshaft speed, and accuracy.
8. Give the two most common types of spearshaft propulsion method.
9. List five types of line material used on line guns.
10. Give three ways to help avoid becoming "caught in the bight".
11. List the five situations where being towed on a line gun by a fish can be dangerous.
12. Name two types of line extending line gun options.
13. What distinguishes a double-barreled gun from a combination gun, both of which carry two spearshafts?
14. T/F With line detached from the spearshaft a hybrid line gun's range, spearshaft speed, and accuracy approach that of a freeshaft gun.

Chapter 4: Hawaiian Slings and Pole Spears

Introduction

Spearguns provide a mechanical release to hold a spear cocked and ready to shoot. Hawaiian slings and pole spears represent non-mechanized release spear delivery systems. To spear a fish with either of these systems the diver manually pulls the spear against the strain of a surgical tubing band and releases it. In the early days of spearfishing, spears were powered using a manual thrusting motion. Some divers used very thin, long, manually thrust spears. These could be extended close to a fish without its noticing until too late. Use of manually powered spears is rare today. Surgical tubing propelled spears have mostly replaced them. Non-mechanical release spears take two forms: pole spears and Hawaiian slings.

Objectives
By the end of this section you should be able to:
1. Understand the difference between spearguns, pole spears, and Hawaiian slings.
2. Know the types of speartips typically used on pole spears.
3. Know the type of configuration which works well for taking large fish with a pole spear.
4. Understand the range limitations with a pole spear.
5. Describe the technique for using a pole spear.
6. Know the type of tip typically used on Hawaiian sling spears and pole spears.
7. Describe the two techniques for using a Hawaiian sling.
8. Explain the advantages to pole spears and Hawaiian slings over mechanical release type spearguns.
9. Explain the disadvantages of pole spears and Hawaiian slings.

Pole Spears

Pole spears are long spears, typically 5 to 7 feet in length. They have a thin-walled surgical tubing power loop attached to one end and a speartip on the other. The spear itself usually consists of two different diameter sections. The stock makes up 4 to 6 feet of the length of a typical pole spear. Stock diameters range from 1/2 to 1 inch, with 5/8 inch most common. The tip extension and speartip make up the final 1 to 2 feet.

The tip extension consists of a 1/4 - 3/8 inch rod, which is typically threaded on each end. One end screws into the pole's stock. The speartip screws onto the other. The extension and speartip combination makes up the part of the pole spear that penetrates the fish.

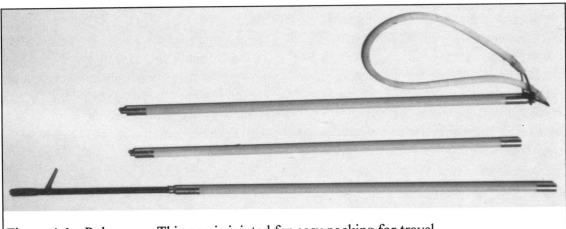

Figure 4-1 - Pole spear. This one is jointed for easy packing for travel.

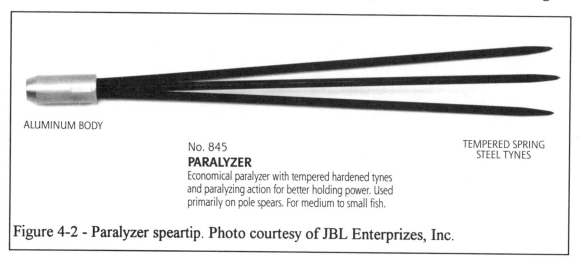

ALUMINUM BODY

No. 845
PARALYZER
Economical paralyzer with tempered hardened tynes
and paralyzing action for better holding power. Used
primarily on pole spears. For medium to small fish.

TEMPERED SPRING
STEEL TYNES

Figure 4-2 - Paralyzer speartip. Photo courtesy of JBL Enterprizes, Inc.

A variety of tips can be used on pole spears. A three pronged "paralyzer" style tip works effectively on fish in the less than ten pound range. Larger fish usually require a single point hinged barb speartip. Trident tips work well on small fish. Detachable tips, especially streamlined models, work well on a wide range of fish sizes. Powerheads, fitted to pole spears, provide protection from predators and allow taking large pelagic fish. For a discussion of various spear tips see **Chapter 5: Special Equipment**.

A technique, borrowed from the outdated manually powered pole spear, involves using a long speartip extension. This sometimes goes unnoticed by the fish, allowing the point of the spear to be positioned close before thrusting. One drawback to long extensions is their tendency to bend under the leverage of a large fish.

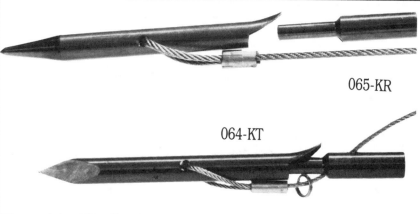

065-KR

064-KT

Figure 4-3 - Slim-line break-away speartip. Note tip retainer ring used for fish removal. Photo courtesy of ABBiller Corporation.

When using a pole spear for large fish, some divers use a break-away float rig. These resemble the rigs used on mechanical release spearguns. The float line secures directly to a detachable tip and leads to a surface float. The diver uses his thumb or a heavy rubber band to hold the line parallel to the spear. After striking a fish the pole pulls away from the tip and the float line releases, leaving the fish tethered to the surface float.

Thrusting a pole spear involves placing the loop over the palm of one hand, the left for a right handed diver, then pulling the pole back with the other hand. Some divers apply a slight twist when pulling the pole back to reduce bend and improve accuracy. Once the pole has been pulled back the diver grips the pole tightly with the loop hand to hold tension until ready to thrust the spear. Releasing the grip of the loop hand propels the spear forward with surprising force. The diver holds onto the power band during the release of the spear to aid in retrieving the fish.

Maximum pole spear range depends upon how far up the spearshaft the loop hand grips the pole. Range typically extends 4 to 5 feet from the end of the tip or about two thirds the length of the spear.

Pole handles, fitted with trigger mechanisms, are available for pole spears. Using a pole handle may not be permitted in countries that do not allow mechanical spearguns. Be sure to verify that they are allowed before using them. The shaft catch mechanism of a pole handle holds the spearshaft with a rubber friction "grip". If you use a pole handle, make sure it grips the pole securely before relying upon it.

As with spearguns, always "shoot" a pole spear while submerged. The elasticity of the power loop can send it back at you without the water's resistance to stop it.

Some divers carry two pole spears while diving. They fit one with a pronged style tip and use it to perform the actual spearing. They fit the other pole spear with a barb-less extension and use it as a stringer. After spearing a fish with the pronged spear, they manually push the "stringer" spear through the fish's gill plate and slide the fish up on the stock of the spear. At the same time that the fish is being "strung" it is removed from the pronged spear. This works especially well with flounder as it rapidly prepares the diver for spearing the next fish.

Hawaiian Slings

Hawaiian slings resemble a combination sling shot and bow and arrow. They consist of a 6 to 14 inch wood or plastic tube to which a surgical tubing power sling attaches. A thin diameter, light weight free spear serves as the spearshaft. The tube is usually 1 to 1 3/4 inches in outside diameter and is sometimes contoured or fitted with a handle to provide an improved grip. A 3/8 to 1/2 inch hole runs through the center of the tube.

As on a pole spear, thin walled surgical tubing provides power for propelling the spearshaft. An aluminum or plastic cap slides onto the tubing to provide a cup into which the blunt end of the spearshaft fits. This provides a grip for the diver and a notch or pocket to hold the spearshaft.

Because the power sling has less power than bands used on mechanical release spearguns, spearshafts for Hawaiian slings are made from thinner diameter rod. They usually consist of steel rod but are sometimes made of aluminum. To reduce weight and bulk, a point is milled into the spearshaft and a single, small hinged barb is attached very near the point. Attaching the small barb close to the tip reduces the depth of penetration needed to engage the barb.

To "shoot" a Hawaiian sling, run the spearshaft through the tube and place the blunt end into the cup on the sling. Pull back the spearshaft, aim, and release. Some divers hold onto the tube as they pull back then release the spearshaft. Others hold the sling and spearshaft just behind the tube. After pulling the spearshaft back, the diver grips the bands and spearshaft tightly. This holds the spearshaft in a "cocked" position, similar to using a pole spear. This technique requires strong hands and fingers, and a pair of gloves.

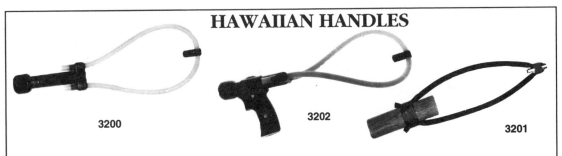

Figure 4-4 - Hawaiian sling handles. Note that the center handle, while shaped like a speargun handle contains no trigger mechanism. Photo courtesy of Sport Diver Manufacturing.

Since Hawaiian slings use freeshafts, kill shots are important. They are typically used on small fish; however, some very large, pelagic fish have been taken with Hawaiian slings. In his book Modern Spearfishing, Vane Ivanovic reports that Jack Ackerman of Hawaii took a 127 pound pompano using a Hawaiian sling (Ivanovic, 1975, pg. 31).

Summary

What are the advantages to pole spears and Hawaiian slings?

They offer simplicity and therefore more mechanical reliability than spearguns. They can be readied for shooting quickly. Pole spears can be readied for another thrust as quickly as the pole can be pulled back. Hawaiian slings take longer since the spearshaft must be retrieved and loaded back into the tube. However, reloading either is quicker than reloading a mechanical release speargun. Both pole spears and Hawaiian slings cost less than mechanical spearguns.

Disadvantages? They lack the range or power of full-sized mechanical spearguns and require more skill.

Due to their simplicity and cost, pole spears and Hawaiian slings make ideal spear systems for beginners. As stated earlier, some countries allow the use of pole spears and Hawaiian slings, but not the use of mechanical spearguns. Some "purest" spearfishermen take pride in and prefer spearfishing with pole spears and Hawaiian slings.

Though pole spears and Hawaiian slings are simple, they warrant the same respect and consideration for safety as a mechanical release spearguns.

Review Questions:
1. What distinguishes a speargun from a pole spear or Hawaiian sling?
2. List three types of speartips used on pole spears.
3. What type of configuration works well for taking large fish with a pole spear?
4. T/F Maximum range on a pole spear is about two thirds the length of the spear.
5. T/F Hawaiian slings have been called the underwater equivalent to combining a sling shot with a bow and arrow.
6. What type of tip is typically used on a Hawaiian sling spear?
7. Briefly describe one technique of using a Hawaiian sling.
8. What are the advantages of pole spears and Hawaiian slings over mechanical release type spearguns?
9. What are the disadvantages of pole spears and Hawaiian slings?

Chapter 5: Special Equipment

Introduction

Choosing the correct spearfishing equipment often makes the difference between a great fish story and a great meal of fresh fish. Previous chapters discussed spear delivery systems and in the process introduced some spearfishing accessory equipment. This chapter explores spearfishing accessory equipment and its use in more detail without repeating information in previous chapters. It includes spearfishing tips that will help your fish story end in a meal of fresh fish.

Objectives
By the end of this section you should be able to:
1. Name the three types of steel typically used in making spearshafts and accessories.
2. Know the effect of spearshaft length on range.
3. Identify spearshaft components.
4. List five types of spearshaft accessories.
5. Understand the importance of keeping accessories firmly tightened.
6. Understand why spearshafts for a one manufacturer's guns should not be used on guns made by another manufacturer.
7. List two spearshaft related problems which can cause missed shots.
8. Identify speartip components.
9. Know the proper way to tighten a speartip or other accessory.
10. Know the situations in which to use a detachable tip.
11. List four types of speartips.
12. Know when powerheads are typically used in spearfishing.
13. Know the effect on range when using a powerhead.
14. Know how a cave diving reel can be used when spearfishing.
15. Describe a toss buoy and know what it is used for.
16. List three devices for carrying game.
17. Know how to use various game carrying devices.
18. Know how and when to use tow sleds.

Spears

Spearshafts are made from either spring stainless steel, stainless steel, or plated non-stainless steel. Stainless, tempered, spring steel makes the best shaft material. This hard material resists bending and the corrosive effect of salt water. Tempering (heat treating) renders post-manufacture modification of these spearshafts difficult. Even simple modifications, like drilling a hole in a tempered spearshaft, will ruin several drill bits. Spring stainless spearshafts exhibit a dark bronze color, which makes freeshafts difficult to locate after being discharged. To remedy this, some manufacturers offer a more highly visible chrome plated freeshaft.

Next in quality as a spearshaft material is non-spring stainless steel. It exhibits high corrosion resistance but lacks the high resilience exhibited by spring stainless. Non-spring stainless is more malleable, allowing easier post-manufacture modification. These spearshafts exhibit a natural nickel color. This makes freeshafts easier to find than the dark colored, non-chrome plated spring stainless models.

Economy spearshafts are made from plated, usually with chromium or zinc, hardened steel. While very strong and more resistant to bending than non-spring stainless, accessories made from this material are prone to corrode when the plating wears. Post-manufacture modification, while relatively easy, breaks through the plating, encouraging corrosion.

The following table summarizes the characteristics of various spearshaft component materials:

Material	Corrosion Resist	Bend Resist	Malleability[1]
Spring Stainless	High	Highest	Low
Stainless	Highest	Moderate	Highest
Plated Steel	Low[2]	High	High

[1] Malleability is the ability of the material to be drilled, threaded, cut, or milled.
[2] Corrosion resistance decreases as the protective plating wears.

Spearshafts come in a variety of types and sizes typically ranging from 24 to over 60 inches. Typical diameters range from 1/4 to 3/8 inches, with a common diameter of 5/16 inch. Longer spearshafts provide longer range. Thicker, heavier spearshafts provide more penetrating force and resist bending when spearing large fish. A standard 60 inch freeshaft fits guns in the 48 to 54 inch size range. With a correctly sized lineshaft, about six inches protrudes from the gun's muzzle.

Some spearshafts, such as lineshafts and pneumatic spearshafts, have threads on one or both ends to provide for affixing speartips, shaft catch adapters, and powerheads. Six millimeter (6 mm) is a common thread size. Some freeshafts and hybrid spearshafts include a 5/16 inch thread milled into their built in spearpoint to allow quick attachment of a powerhead. Seven millimeter represents another commonly found shaft thread. For components that do not fit a given thread, adapters are available; however, adapters add to the weight and bulk of the shaft.

Shaft catch notches on spearshafts are not standard. Guns from different manufacturers use different catch notch designs. Some spearshaft catch notches are milled flat or contain grooves to help keep the spearshaft from twisting in the gun's catch mechanism. Even if they seem to fit and hold, spearshafts should not be used interchangeably between guns unless they are of the same design. Using the wrong spearshaft in a gun could result in the spearshaft twisting off the catch and firing accidentally.

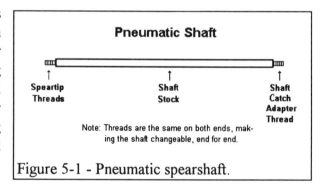

Pneumatic Shaft

Speartip Threads   Shaft Stock   Shaft Catch Adapter Thread

Note: Threads are the same on both ends, making the shaft changeable, end for end.

Figure 5-1 - Pneumatic spearshaft.

Pneumatic gun spearshafts differ from most band gun spearshafts in that they do not have cocking notches built into the spearshaft. They usually carry threads on both ends. Just as with a typical band gun spearshaft, one end takes a speartip. A shaft catch adapter screws onto the other end. While rare, some band gun spearshafts also conform to this double thread arrangement.

Note that the shaft includes no line slide stop. On most pneumatic spearshaft designs the flare of the adapter serves as both the shaft catch notch and the line stop. Always ensure that adapters are screwed on solidly and set with thread locking glue.

Spearshaft durability

When is a spearshaft no longer of service? Shafts occasionally break or bend. A broken spearshaft is obviously unusable. When a spearshaft breaks, which rarely happens, it typically occurs at a weak point such as a drill through hole, at a band cocking notch, or at the speartip thread. Shafts which have been retrieved after several weeks under salt water are particularly susceptible to breaking. Even "stainless" steel deteriorates.

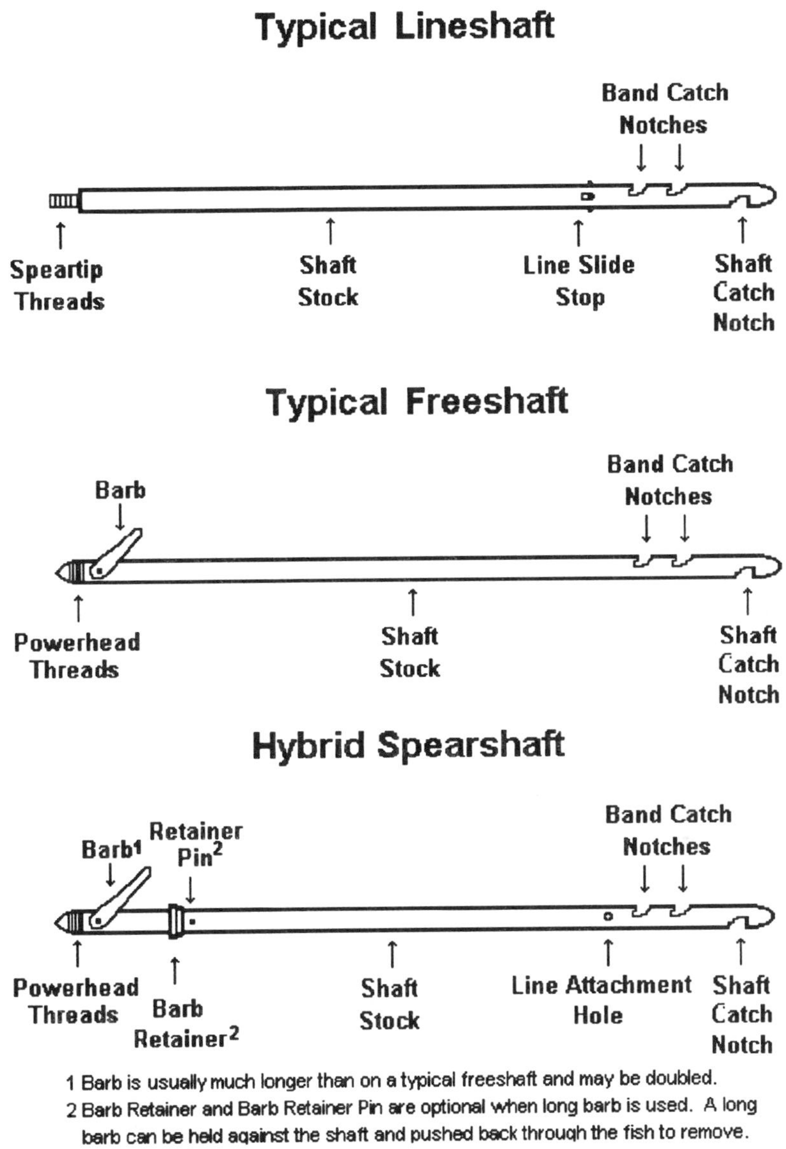

A large fish or a strain at an odd angle can bend a spearshaft. Bent spearshafts are unusable because they will not track straight. It is usually best to retire bent spearshafts. Even slightly bent spearshafts can rarely be straightened. To check a spearshaft for straightness, roll it on a flat surface such as a counter top or a level floor. A spearshaft can also be checked for straightness by spinning it like a top with the point resting on a hard surface while holding it with a line slide. If the spearshaft wobbles it is bent.

Typical Lineshaft

Band Catch Notches

Speartip Threads — Shaft Stock — Line Slide Stop — Shaft Catch Notch

Typical Freeshaft

Barb

Band Catch Notches

Powerhead Threads — Shaft Stock — Shaft Catch Notch

Hybrid Spearshaft

Barb[1]   Retainer Pin[2]

Band Catch Notches

Powerhead Threads   Barb Retainer[2] — Shaft Stock — Line Attachment Hole — Shaft Catch Notch

1 Barb is usually much longer than on a typical freeshaft and may be doubled.
2 Barb Retainer and Barb Retainer Pin are optional when long barb is used. A long barb can be held against the shaft and pushed back through the fish to remove.

Figure 5-2 - Though not to scale, the diagrams above show typical lineshaft, freeshaft, and hybrid spearshaft features.

Sighting down a spearshaft can be dangerous so is not recommended. Always verify, when loading a spearshaft in your gun, that it lies straight and evenly in the gun's spearshaft guide. A bent spearshaft causes misses on relatively easy shots.

Just as a bent spearshaft causes inaccuracy, severely bent barbs can also throw off the trajectory of a spearshaft. Some freeshafts come with barbs with slight bends on the very end. This feature aids the barbs in opening up when the shaft is pulled backward in a fish. However, an excessively bent barb or one which does not fold up parallel to the spearshaft, causes inaccuracy. A severely deformed or bent barb indicates weakness and could result in loosing a fish. Always inspect barbs as you load your gun. Carry spare spearshafts and speartips to replace questionable ones.

Figure 5-3 - This shaft was bent fighting a large fish.

Refer to the discussion under **Gun Configurations** in **Chapter 3: Spearguns,** to the **Glossary,** and to **Chapter 6: Technique** for additional information on the application of various types of spearshafts.

Spearshaft Accessories

Spearshaft accessories, such as line slides, spear tips, and adapters, are available in stainless or plated steel. Other materials used for speargun accessories, include brass, bronze, and plastic. Various accessories available for spearshafts include:

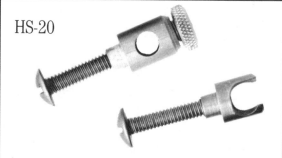

Figure 5-4 - Spare shaft holder. Photo courtesy of AB Biller Company.

- Spare spearshaft holders, which attach to the sides of spearguns to allow carrying extra spearshafts;
- Line slides, to which line gun line is attached;
- Line slide backing plates, that slide on a spearshaft between the line slide and the line slide stop. These reduce wear on the slide and slide stop;
- Hinged barb hold-down retainers, that aid in removing a spearshaft from a fish. These come standard on most screw on speartips.
- Shaft pins, that attach hinged barbs and serve as slide stops;
- Speartips and powerheads (See *Speartips* in this chapter);
- Thread adapters, used to convert one thread size to another;
- Shaft catch adapters, to convert double end threaded spearshafts to a particular manufacturer's shaft catch design.

STAINLESS	BRASS
3475 - Standard to 6MM	**3470** - Standard to 6MM
3476 - 5/16 to 6MM	**3471** - 6MM to Standard
3477 - 7MM to 6MM	**3472** - 6MM to 7MM
	3473 - 7MM to 6MM

Figure 5-5 - Thread adapters. Photo courtesy of Sport Divers Manufacturing.

What are some common problems with spearshaft accessories?

Accessories which screw onto spearshafts deserve particular attention. The constant concussion of the spearshaft being fired will eventually loosen a securely tightened speartip or other screw-on accessory. Besides causing thread wear, a loose accessory can result in lost equipment and lost fish. Only tighten screw-on accessories with the spearshaft removed from the gun.

PNEUMATIC ADAPTERS, SS
▼ D221 - D225

GSD   Nemrod   Technisub

Cressi   Mares

Figure 5-6 - Various screw-on pneumatic adapters. Courtesy of Marine Diving Equipment.

Line slides can jam on lineshafts. Worn or split slide stops or line slides cause this. Line stops become beveled with repeated firing. The line slide can wedge on a worn, beveled stop. Cracked line slides also cause jams. Splitting occurs more frequently with solid metal line slides than with the coiled spring slides. A crack in a slide allows the slide to ride up on the slide stop, resulting in a jammed slide.

Regardless of the cause, a jammed line slide can usually be freed by guiding the back of the spearshaft into the muzzle and bumping the slide against the muzzle. For severely jammed slides, tapping with the back edge of a dive knife will usually free the slide. This is a temporary solution and the line slide stop should be filed square with the spearshaft body or the line slide replaced, according to the cause for the jam.

A split line slide can be temporarily "fixed" by removing the speartip and reversing the line slide so that the non-split side strikes the line stop. To properly correct this problem replace the line slide.

Speartips

Speartips come in several designs. The most common is a screw-on, single point tip with single or double barbs. Multiple point tips such as flat fork and paralyzer tips are popular for pole spears. Detachable or break-away tips are used primarily for large fish although, some polespear hunters use them on small fish. Some spearshafts, such as freeshafts and hybrid spearshafts, include spearpoints milled directly into them with barbs mounted directly on their shaft stocks.

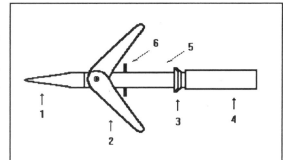

Figure 5-7 - 1) 1) Spearpoint; 2) Barb; 3) Barb retainer; 4) Threaded collar; 5) Speartip shaft; 6) Barb spreader.

Like any screw-on accessory, a speartip should be firmly tightened. Before tightening, remove the spearshaft from the gun. This prevents damage to the gun's shaft catch housing. Tighten the speartip by using two pair of pliers, preferably locking pliers (Figure 7-3). Adding thread locking glue helps keep the tip threaded securely to the spearshaft, but, even with glue speartips warrant periodic checking. (Refer to the section on speartip maintenance in **Chapter 7: Spearfishing Safety** for additional safety considerations with speartips.)

Single point, hinged-barb speartips

Single point speartips come in a variety of designs. Some have round spearpoints while others have beveled, angular points. Round spearpoints are typically used in rocky, hard surface terrain as they resist dulling from impact and are relatively easy to re-sharpen. Restoring the point on a round spearpoint requires grinding a relatively small, conical shaped surface area. Beveled, angular tips penetrate better than round tips. They work best in open water or areas where dulling from impact is unlikely. These points carry more cutting edges. Restoring the point and edges on these requires uniformly filing or grinding each flat surface.

Some speartips allow switching between spearpoint types. These speartips have a threaded protrusion ahead of the barbs on the front of the tip shaft. Spearpoints can be threaded onto the

SPEAR TIPS

3463 - Single Barb - Small - 6MM
3464 - Single Barb - Large - 6MM
3465 - Double Barb - 6MM
3466 - Double Barb Detachable - 6MM

Figure 5-8 - Speartips: Double barb, double barb detachable, single barb. Photo courtesy of Sport Divers Manufacturing.

threaded protrusion to match spearpoint with terrain and quarry. As with the speartip itself, always remove the spearshaft from the gun before changing spearpoints.

Single point speartips come with single or multiple hinged barbs (flippers). A barb or tip swivel feature, available with some models, helps prevent fish from tearing off the spearshaft. Barbs are usually held open by a barb spreader. A spreader typically consists of a cross section of surgical tubing or rubber stem mounted near the barb's hinge. Some speartip models use springs to hold the barbs open; however, springs require more maintenance.

A barb retainer holds down hinged barbs when removing fish. The retainer consists of a flared ring that slides freely on the tip shaft. When hunting, the barbs are usually left free to protrude, held out slightly by the spreader. After a fish is speared, the speartip is pushed through the fish. The flared part of the ring holds the ends of the barbs against the tip shaft while backing the spearshaft out of the fish. Once removed from the fish the retainer ring is pulled off the barbs before reloading the spearshaft.

The spearshaft coupling is a threaded collar at the back end of tip shaft and screws onto the spearshaft. When not screwed onto a spearshaft, keep debris out of the threaded hole in the coupling. Debris on either the coupling or spearshaft will cause thread abrasion when the speartip is screwed onto the spearshaft. Clean both before joining them. Avoid oil and other lubricants as they invite a loose speartip.

Detachable tips

Detachable or "slip" tips (Figure 4-3) slide over or into a detachable tip holder or directly onto the end of the spearshaft. A short length of cable attaches the tip to the spearshaft. This provides enough slack so that, after penetrating a fish, the tip can pull from the holder and remain in the fish. Only the cable protrudes from the entry hole in the fish. This reduces the likelihood of the fish tearing off by eliminating the leverage on the spearshaft. (See **Chapter 4: Hawaiian Slings & Pole Spears**.)

Detachable tips are primarily used on pelagic fish, such as amberjack and tuna, and with fish in the thirty-plus pound range. They are sometimes used on smaller, soft fleshed fish as well. However, the time required to remove fish from detachable tips makes them less desirable for smaller fish.

Multiple point tips

Multiple point tips enjoy popularity with pole spears and for shooting small fish. There are three basic styles: paralyzer, flat fork, and trident.

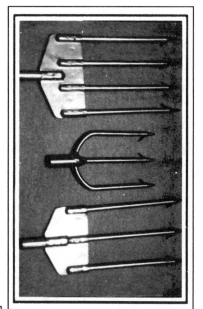

▲TIPS, FLAT FORK
D420 - Tip, flat, 6mm, 4 prong
D416 - Tip, hinged, 6mm,
D419 - Tip, flat, 6mm, 3 prong

Figure 5-9 - Flat fork spear-tips. Courtesy Marine Diving Equipment Manufacturing.

Paralyzer tips (Figure 4-2) consist of three or four thin, spring stainless steel, sharpened prongs. These usually un-barbed prongs are joined together and flair slightly away from each other as they extend out toward the points. The sharpened prongs are fairly straight. As they penetrate a fish, besides the likelihood of one of the prongs striking a kill spot, the prongs spread, wedging the fish on the tip. They usually

No. 865
TRIDENT POINT
Low maintenance barbed point used for medium to small fish on polespear or reef gun.

Figure 5-10 - Trident speartip. Courtesy JBL Enterprises.

disable the fish, hence, the name "paralyzer".

Flat fork tips are constructed of several straight, sharpened, fixed-barb prongs joined together by a flat plate or onto each other with welds. While they do not have the same disabling effect of the spreading prongs of a paralyzer tip, the multiple prongs increase the likelihood of hitting a kill spot. The fixed barbs hold the fish once the prongs penetrate. Flat fork tips work best on small fish and flat fish, such as flounder.

Trident tips are similar to flat fork tips. Instead of being positioned flat, they are bent into a three dimensional, triangular pattern. They have a similar effect and are used on basically the same type of fish as flat fork tips.

Powerheads

Powerheads illicit the most controversy among the various speartip types. As protection against large predators they enjoy almost undisputed acceptance, but as a means for taking fish they suffer for support. Some feel that they are too effective, providing an unfair advantage to the spearfisherman. Others feel that powerheads provide the safest, most humane, and selective method of taking large fish. This section describes powerheads and explains their use. It defers judgment of powerheads to the individual sportsperson. Also, see **Chapter 7: Spearfishing Safety** for safe powerhead practices.

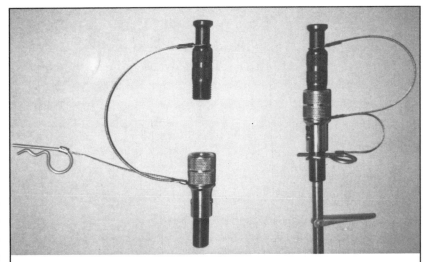

Figure 5-11 - Low profile .223 caliber powerhead. Photo on right shows powerhead assembled with safety (ring clip) in place and mounted on a threaded point spearshaft.

What is a powerhead? A powerhead is a cylindrical steel chamber with a firing pin. It threads onto to a spearshaft or attaches with a set screw slip collar. An ammunition cartridge loads into the chamber. The cartridge discharges when the spear strikes a fish, providing a very effective knock-out concussion for killing large fish.

A powerhead consists of: 1) A cylindrical steel cartridge chamber, 2) A firing pin, 3) A safety, and, 4) A coupling for attaching the powerhead to a spearshaft, "bang stick", or speargun powerhead holder. According to federal regulation, a powerhead should be attached to a shaft or rod that exceeds an overall length of 26 inches, when measured from the firing pin to the end of the rod. To meet this regulation some manufacturers sell powerheads tack welded onto a rod. Follow manufacturers' recommendations on using and handling powerheads to avoid conflict with federal regulations and for safe powerhead use.

A powerhead's cartridge chamber opens for loading, using either a slip fit or screw-on fitting. With the slip fit, "O" rings typically provide a friction seal, keeping the chamber closed. Chamber diameter and length vary with caliber of cartridge used. Common calibers include .38, .44 magnum, .223, and .357. Some powerheads use shotgun shells. The size of the load, not the caliber of the projectile, determines a powerheads effective power. The expanding gases, released on detonation, create a damaging concussion. Thus, a .223, with its large load but small projectile, delivers a highly effective blow.

There are three methods for attaching a powerhead to the spearshaft: 1) Threaded coupling; 2) Thumb screw; 3) Slip fit. Like standard speartips, most powerheads have internal threads for screwing directly onto the end of a spearshaft. A more versatile attachment uses a thumb operated setscrew for holding the powerhead in place. This provides a less secure attachment than a threaded coupling but fits a wider range of spearshafts and speartips.

A powerhead can also attach to a hand held pole (bang stick) or a special gun mounted powerhead holder. Both the bang stick or gun mounted holder rely upon a strong manual thrust to discharge the cartridge when confronted by a predator. The safety is left in place until needed.

The spearshaft usually extends forward of a gun mounted powerhead. (See Figure 5-12, - Speargun with powerhead mount (left) and spare spearshaft mount (right). Photo courtesy of AB Biller.) To ready the powerhead for firing either the shaft must be removed or the powerhead extended beyond the spear. Discharging the spearshaft offers the fastest method of clearing the powerhead. Some powerhead mounts provide thumb screws which loosen to allow sliding the mount forward in its holder.

Most powerheads have an integral firing pin. However, special powerheads, generically referred to as personal protection devices (PPDs), slip on over the spearpoint. With these powerheads the spearpoint serves as the firing pin. Since they mount on a spear when needed for protection and rely upon the spearpoint for a firing pin, they have no safety. When a PPD is on the end of a spearshaft it is ready to fire. Therefore they should only be installed when needed and removed as soon as possible.

When used properly, powerheads take large fish efficiently and safely. In order for the firing pin to strike the cartridge's primer cap the powerhead must strike solidly against the fish. Upon impact the discharge from the cartridge injures the fish, and, if the powerhead strikes the head or other vital area, incapacitates it. A fish struck a glancing blow or in a non-vital area can still escape. This occurs when the cartridge fails to detonate or if the fish is not incapacitated. From a diving safety view, a large fish, stunned or killed by a powerhead poses less danger to the diver than a large, lively fish on a lineshaft.

Some bcds have small pockets, ideal for carrying powerheads. Individual, add-on pockets are also available. Most divers carry their powerhead in a pocket reserved exclusively for this purpose. A powerhead pocket should close securely, yet allow easy access. Because of their weight and small size, powerheads are easily lost. Carrying powerheads in pockets shared with other gear invites their loss. Since it is seldom needed for protection, you may not miss your powerhead until after a dive.

As stated in **Chapter 7: Spearfishing Safety**, powerheads should be loaded and unloaded in the water. However, some divers carry loaded powerheads in the lapel of their wetsuit jacket. This is dangerous. A lapel carried powerhead can easily fall to the deck as the diver removes his jacket. A dropped powerhead can accidentally

Figure 5-12

discharge when it strikes a hard surface. Always treat powerheads with respect. Never rely completely on the safety to keep them from discharging. Refer to **Chapter 7: Spearfishing Safety** for additional powerhead safety practices.

Powerheads are much heavier and bulkier than conventional screw on speartips. The added weight and bulk reduce effective shooting range to about one and one half spearshaft lengths from the end of the speargun.. This renders powerheads ineffective on elusive fish. Also, the discharge from a powerhead causes significantly more damage to the fish, making them less desirable for use on small fish. Like with standard spear tips, make head shots to avoid damaging the meaty part of the fish.

Technique with a powerhead resembles that of spearfishing with a line gun. For security and simplicity, a powerhead usually attaches to a lineshaft with a threaded coupling. Because of the limited range imposed by the extra weight and bulk of the powerhead, only one loop of shooting slack is typically used. In deep, open water divers try to shoot fish from a slight angle below the fish. This enables them to retrieve stunned, sinking fish with minimum depth exposure.

Spearfishermen who use powerheads for taking multiple fish on a single dive sometimes stash extra cartridges in their wetsuit sleeves. Keeping extra cartridges handy speeds reloading. This does not present the same danger as carrying a powerhead inside of the wetsuit lapel. Loose cartridges do not have a firing pin poised to strike their primer cap. However, do not let cartridges fall to the deck. Handle them carefully.

A few tips will help when spearfishing with a powerhead. Apply nail polish or enamel to the primer cap and other areas of potential leaks on the cartridge. This minimizes powder wetting leaks. Another good practice is to retire and safely dispose of un-spent cartridges after a day of diving. This reduces "dud" cartridges. Using them at a firing range in a conventional firearm provides a good way to dispose of used cartridges. Be sure to rinse used cartridges and allow them to thoroughly air dry before using them in a conventional firearm.

A powerhead with too weak of a spring may discharge upon being fired from a speargun. To correct this, return the powerhead to the retailer for replacement of the spring or with a different model powerhead with a stronger spring.

Figure 5-13 - Speargun line reel. This composite reel has a quick mount/ dismount plate. Courtesy AB Biller Company.

Never discharge a powerhead against a piling, ledge, or other solid object. This damages the cartridge chamber and results in jammed cartridge casings. The discharge of the cartridge can also propel the spearshaft back toward you. For the same reasons never discharge a powerhead out of water. For additional information on powerheads refer to **Chapter 7: Spearfishing Safety** and the manufacturer's instructions.

Reels: types, technique
There are two types of line reels used in spearfishing: Speargun reels and cave diving reels:

Figure 5-14 - **Heavy duty aluminum reel manufactured by TJS.**

- **Gun reels** are heavily constructed and use strong line to take the strain of a pulling fish;
- **Cave reels** are lightly built and carry lighter line used as an aid to underwater navigation.

Both types of reel serve a purpose spearfishing. Refer to the discussion on line gun reels in **Chapter 3: Spearguns** for additional information.

Reels attach differently depending upon whether they are mounted on wooden or metal guns. Screw mount or bolt reels directly onto wooden guns. Use hose clamps on metal guns to avoid penetrating the sealed barrel.

Cave reels also prove useful to spearfishermen. Used in their traditional fashion, a diver secures one end of the line to a point of reference. He then pays out line to assure that he can return to the point of reference. Avoid the use of cave reels to penetrate wrecks or caves until after obtaining proper training.

Cave reels can also be used during safety stops to help the boat operator locate and stay with a group of divers. In strong current, a surface float is not always practical due to water depth or strong current. In addition, surface floats can hinder spearfishing activity. However, at the end of a dive a lift bag or other inflatable float can be secured to the cave reel line and released to the surface. The float allows the boat to easily locate and follow the divers as they drift with the current during their safety stop.

FLOAT BALLS

Measurement given is total inches around outside of ball.

1372 - 20"   **1375** - 30"   **1376** - 40"
1377 - 50"   **1378** - 60"

Figure 5-16 - Float buoy. Photo courtesy of Sport Divers Manufacturing.

Drift dive floats

Basic technique for diving in current also applies to spearfishing. When possible, divers should carry a drift dive float. Large, orange inflatable fishing buoys work well for use as dive floats. A length of floating polypropylene rope, at least twice the water's depth in length, makes good drift buoy line. During the dive, a lead diver carries the float line attached to a small anchor. A dive weight or blunt ended grapnel makes a good anchor. An anchor allows the lead diver to temporarily anchor the float to spear or string a fish. The other divers maintain visual contact with the lead diver. At the end of the dive they surface together. When spearfishing with a drift dive float, avoid tangling speargun line around the float line.

Float lines

When diving in current from an anchored boat, trail a float line of at least 75 feet from the back of the boat. Use floating polypropylene line with a large float on the end. A length of water ski rope and a large, orange inflatable fishing buoy make an ideal combination for float lines. Divers should dive by swimming into the current until ready to return to the boat.

Because divers sometimes "miss the boat," a loud whistle and a highly visible

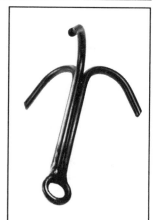

5414 - Drift Anchor
Small - 7" x 5/16"

Figure 5-17 - Grapnel style drift anchor. Photo courtesy of Sport Divers Manufacturing.

surface marker should be carried by each diver. For a diver on the surface a plastic garbage bag makes an excellent surface marker. It can be folded flat and easily stowed in a bcd pocket. On the surface it can be manually inflated to make the diver more visible. Most garbage bags come in white but large, orange jack-o-lantern bags show up better.... You just have to wait until the Halloween season to buy them. Be sure to prevent plastic bags from "escaping" into the environment.

Toss buoy

Spearfishing demands efficient use of in-water time. One of the subtle keys to efficient diving includes accurately targeting a site by marking it with a buoy prior to a dive. A dive site marked with a simple toss buoy allows divers to descend down the buoy line, directly onto the target site. This reduces in-water search time.

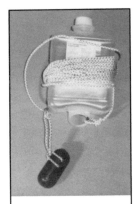

You can make toss buoys from a plastic half-gallon bottle, with an appropriate length of heavy line and small weight attached. Attach the bottle to one end of the line; the weight to the other. Wind the line around the bottle for storage.

When tossed into the water, the line unwinds from the bottle, lowering the anchor weight to the bottom. Select a bottle with flat or slightly indented, rather than rounded, sides. The flat or indented sides provide a good surface to help keep the line from slipping off the end of the bottle during deployment. Fill the bottle with insulating foam, available from most hardware stores, to keep the bottle from sinking when it develops leaks.

Figure 5-18 - Toss buoy.

Use strong line to help when retrieving fouled weights. The amount of weight you use depends upon depth, current, and weather. One or two pounds usually works well.

Divers often keep several buoys with lines measured for various depths. Line should measure at least one fourth longer than the expected water depth. Too short of a line will prevent the weight from reaching bottom. To guard against this watch the buoy as it unwinds. If it bobs when all of the line unwinds the anchor weight did not reach the bottom. Even if the weight reaches bottom, too short of a line will allow the weight to drag along the bottom. If the line is too long the buoy will not sit over the marked spot; however, it is better for the line to be too long than too short.

Use toss marker buoys to mark "breaks" and "fish shows", which often indicate good dive sites. When a good spot shows on the boat's electronic depth recorder, toss the buoy over the stern. Putting divers into the water and retrieving them takes precious time. Circle the boat around the buoy several times and verify the spot before anchoring or diving.

Freedivers sometimes use toss marker buoys as place markers to maintain position over a good dive spot in murky water. Before a breath-hold dive, the weight on the end of the marker line can be hauled up and used to help carry the freediver to the bottom. The diver carries the weight along during the dive and, upon finding a spot of interest, drops the weight. After resting on the surface, the diver then follows the line to the weight. This guides the diver directly to the spot and avoids loss of precious bottom time. The float doubles as a holder for fish stringers, dive flags, and other spare gear. As with any line, avoid becoming entangled.

Scuba divers sometimes carry small marker buoys in a bcd pocket. These often prove valuable for marking a spot found during a dive. The weight is placed on the spot and the buoy allowed to un-wind and ascend to the surface so that the position can be accurately marked on the boat's Loran or GPS.

Stringers and game bags

Safety pin style stringers, line stringers, and game bags comprise the most common means for carrying fish. (See **Chapter 4: Hawaiian Slings and Pole Spears Pole** for description of a method for using a pole spear as a fish stringer.) Stringing or bagging your catch keeps it under control until you remove it from the water. String or bag your fish as soon as possible after spearing. To avoid loosing your fish, string or bag it before removing the spearshaft. A stunned fish sometimes revives when the shaft is removed.

Maintaining control of the fish is critical no matter which stringing device you use. Consider the various types and styles and select the one appropriate for your hunting style.

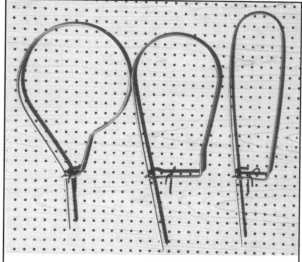

Figure 5-19 - Exposed point safety pin style stringers.

Safety pin stringers consist of a stainless steel rod, bent so that it will clip back into itself. Safety pin stringers come with either an exposed point or protected point. With the exposed point design string fish by running the exposed point through the fish's gills or eyes before unclipping it. After un-clipping, slide the fish onto the loop, and re-clip it. Some safety pin stringers keep the point tucked away in a stainless cover. This keeps the point from causing damage or accidental injury, but slows the fish stringing process.

When choosing a safety pin stringer, ensure that the point remains secured in the retainer and does not accidentally disengage when loaded with a heavy catch. Stringers constructed of small gauge rod and some non-exposed point stringers unclip too easily. Choose heavy gauge stringers to eliminate this problem.

Figure 5-20 - Line stringer. Photo courtesy of AB Biller Company.

Line stringers consist of a length of line with a metal ring attached to one end and a sharp metal rod (fid) attached to the other. To string your first fish, run the fid through the first fish's gills or eyes then loop the line through the ring. String subsequent fish by simply running the fid through their gills or eyes. The first fish serves as a stop on the end of he stringer. Stringing fish is fast with line stringers and they are effective in controlling small and dead fish.

Game bags serve equally well for fish, other game, and collectible items. Placing fish in a bag hides it from predators. A bag does not prevent the scent of your speared fish from escaping into the water; however, some predators react to the sight of injured fish. Some divers stow a draw-string game bag in their bcd pocket for use when they encounter a lobster or other bag-able "treasure".

Avoid allowing previously shot and bagged fish do to escape, when bagging game. To prevent this, twist the bag above the already bagged game prior to opening it.

Which type of game carrying device is best?

Your choice of game carrying device depends primarily upon the size of fish you hunt. Safety pin style stringers hold virtually any size of fish; however, you can not legally string lobster. Game bags are primarily used with smaller fish and shell fish. Line stringers provide an efficient means for stringing but do not offer the same amount of control as a safety pin stringer or game bag.

Figure 5-21 - Various game bags.

Sleds

Diver tow sleds, also called planers, enjoy popularity in searching for dive spots. A typical sled consists of an oval plastic or plywood board with hand hold cutouts. A polypropylene ski rope is tied between the sled and the boat. A snorkeler tows behind the boat, using the sled as a planer to descend and ascend. Sleds allow divers to search a large area of bottom with little swimming effort. Their effective use depends upon water clarity, water depth, and diver skill.

While popular, tow sleds demand particular caution. Sleds should never be used by divers on scuba, only by snorkelers. A scuba diver using a sled can easily ascend too rapidly, inviting an air expansion or other injury. In addition, since a scuba diver stays below the surface, it is difficult to tell when the diver releases from the sled. Consequently, when the scuba diver releases it can go un-noticed by the boat operators.

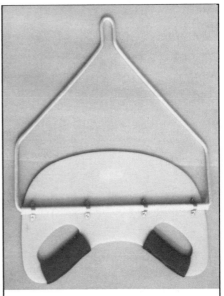

When towing snorkelers a spotter should constantly watch the divers. A water skiing type of rearview mirror will help the boat operator keep track of the divers. Toss buoys, towed by the snorkelers, will help the spotter determine when a submerged snorkeler drops off from the sled. They can also be used by the diver to mark a spot of interest.

Figure 5-22 - Plastic tow sled.

Towing two sleds is safer and more efficient than towing one. Divers can work as a team by alternately diving below the surface. Having one diver below and the other on the surface reduces gaps in area coverage in murky water and keeps one diver resting and watching from the surface.

When operating the boat, avoid tangling the boat prop in the tow and buoy lines or hitting the divers. To help towing go smoothly, agree on hand signals between the boat operator and the divers to indicate:

- Speed up
- Slow down
- Stop
- Pick-up
- Gear needs, e.g. net, tickle stick, speargun, etc.

Due to the complication of the towing process, divers should not tow while carrying spearguns. Establish a signal to have the boat circle around and bring one to the diver when needed.

Computers

While not specifically spearfishing equipment, dive computers deserve mention due to their efficiency in tracking repetitive dives. Spearfishing typically entails more dives, of shorter duration, during a dive day than most other types of diving. Computers reduce human error by simplifying dive planning. During and between dives computers automatically track and compute allowable no decompression stop bottom time at various depths. Most of them also provide allowance for multi-level diving. This results in relatively longer allowable no decompression stop bottom time.

A computer serves only as well as the algorithm on which it is based. Research available models before selecting one that suits your diving style. Then follow safe diving practice and the computer's instructions. The Bibliography lists computer related books and publications to help in choosing a computer. Recommendation: Choose a conservative computer; then use it conservatively.

Summary

Just like with spearguns, the myriad of available spearfishing accessory equipment makes spearfishing a highly individual sport. The type of equipment you select depends upon:

- Species and size of fish
- Type of underwater terrain
- Water depth and condition
- Dive platform
- Local laws
- Price

It also depends upon your ability and personal preference. Which ever combination of spearguns and accessories you select, perfect your ability to use your equipment. Stay in tune with the accessory market by visiting dive centers in various areas and by talking to other spearfishermen. You may discover an innovative technique by combining two other techniques.

Review Questions:
1. Name the three types of metal typically used in spearshafts and accessories.
2. T/F Longer spearshafts are used for longer range. Heavier spearshafts are used for larger fish.
3. List five types of spear accessories.
4. Why is it important to keep accessories firmly tightened?
5. Why should spearshafts for guns made by one manufacturer not be used on guns made by another manufacturer?
6. List two spearshaft related problems which can cause missed shots.
7. Match speartip components to the following diagram:

Point _____

Barbs _____

Barb spreader _____

Barb retainer _____

Tip shaft _____

Threaded collar _____

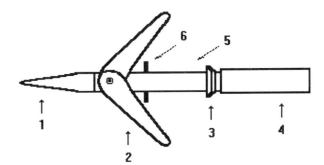

8. How should a speartip or other accessory be tightened on a spearshaft?
9. Generally when are detachable tips used?
10. List four types of speartips.
11. In spearfishing, on what type of fish are powerheads generally used.
12. When used on a line gun, what is the effect on the gun's range when using a powerhead.
13. How can a cave diving reel be used during a safety stop?
14. What is a toss buoy?
15. List three devices for carrying game.
16. Is a fish removed from the spearshaft before or after the fish is on the stringer?
17. Why should tow sleds not be used by divers on scuba?

Chapter 6: Technique

Introduction

Spearfishing technique varies according to the gear used and...personal preference. Other chapters address spearfishing technique relating to gun configuration and accessory spearfishing equipment. This chapter covers general spearfishing technique. Individual spearfishermen match equipment and technique to the type of fish that they pursue, the spearfishing environment, and their ability. Technique presented in this chapter establishes the foundation for helping you develop an effective and creative personal style.

Objectives
By the end of this section you should be able to:
1. Explain why a "check list" is important when preparing for a dive trip.
2. State the purpose of a float plan.
3. State the purpose for marking measurements on your speargun.
4. Define the terms "kill shot" and "stone shot".
5. Explain how to keep a floating gun under control.
6. Explain how to subdue a small fighting fish.
7. Explain how to subdue medium and large fish.
8. State the precaution to take before reaching under a ledge to retrieve a "holed up" fish.
9. Describe the effect of a fish's swim bladder on a diver's buoyancy when surfacing.
10. Explain how to deal with a stringer of fish that is causing you to ascend too fast.
11. Define "ranging".
12. Describe how buddy pairs can swim safely together when spearfishing.

Pre-dive Organization

Proper technique begins with pre-dive trip organization. This includes verifying that your dive, spearfishing, and personal gear is complete and in good working order. Except for the addition of spearfishing gear, preparing for a spearfishing outing resembles preparation for any other diving activity. Many basic dive manuals address the details of dive trip planning and preparation. However, the check list provided below will help keep you from forgetting a vital piece of gear or preparation details. Use it as a seed list from which to build your own pre-dive trip check list:

- Directions to dive site (charts, LORAN or GPS numbers, tide and current tables, etc.)
- Current weather and water condition report
- Mask
- Fins & booties
- Snorkel
- Weight belt and weights
- Filled tanks
- Regulator
- bcd
- Catch net, tickle stick, and gauge (for lobster)

- Exposure suit
- Speargun(s) with spare spearshafts, tips, and bands
- Dive computer or dive tables
- At least one underwater flashlight with fresh batteries
- Spare parts kit with tools
- Gloves
- Stringer
- Game bag
- Dive knife
- Filet knife
- Fishing license with appropriate stamps, e.g. lobster stamp
- Dive log
- Ice chest with ice for fish
- Ice chest with food, snacks, and drink
- Dry clothes, towels, etc.
- Foul weather gear (to wear over exposure suit between dives)
- Hat
- Sun glasses
- Sun screen
- Money
- First aid kit
- File a float plan

Pack as compactly as possible. Most spearfishing is done from boats with limited storage space and a shortage of dry storage. Use water tight bags for clothes. Consolidate ice chests. Use gear bags for dive gear. Mark your dive and personal gear, including dive weights, with your name or initials.

File a float plan so that someone on shore knows when you expect to return, a description of the boat, and the general vicinity of where you plan to dive. Instruct this person on who to contact in the event that you are overdue. (Be sure to communicate with your contact person by telephone or radio if you change your plan.)

A good divemaster course will help the prospective spearfisherman with dive planning and organization. The rest of this chapter offers tips and recommendations aimed at improving spearfishing effectiveness and safety.

Mark measurements on gun

Some spearfishermen mark key measurements on their gun to assist in assessing fish size underwater. An underwater reference puts size into perspective and helps eliminate shooting undersized fish. Paint or dive gear markers works well for this purpose.

Figure 6-1 - Speargun showing marks at 10", 12", and 20".

Spotting a fish to shoot

"OK, My skills are up to snuff and I've got my gun and equipment... Where are the fish?"

Some species of prized and edible fish make themselves obvious to divers. In the Southern United States, hogfish and sheepshead are good examples. This does not necessarily mean that they are easily taken. They sometimes seem to sense danger and make imperceptible but effective moves to avoid being positioned in front of the speargun. Other fish, such as grouper and California's calico bass, are more difficult to spot and bring within range. One key to successful spearfishing is to avoid appearing as a threat. Stalking technique for wary fish includes:

- Enter the water quietly. Avoid giant stride and back roll entries, especially in shallow water.
- Swim and move casually. Fish can out swim you and jerky motion frightens them.
- Hold your gun down, which you should do anyway for safety, until within range for a shot. Then calmly and smoothly bring the gun on target by extending the gun and sighting along the spearshaft before shooting. Again, avoid rapid and jerky motions, which will frighten the fish.
- Fish sometimes swim fairly close to you but avoid the speargun. Try stopping and resting the gun in a position so that the fish swim in front of it.
- Swim parallel to a wary fish's path; Avoid eye contact until within range; Then calmly turn, aim, and shoot.
- Use vegetation, rock outcrops, wreckage, or baitfish for cover.
- Look under ledges. Use a flashlight to peer into holes and crevices.
- Lay down a stringer of already taken fish, swim away for a few minutes and then come back to it. The stringer of fish sometimes draws other fish.

Even using the above techniques, taking your first fish may prove difficult. Maintain your patience. You will succeed. Avoid the temptation to shoot an undersized or illegal fish. This practice gives spearfishing a bad reputation. Which fish species you target for your first game depends upon the local offing. Pick one of the easier targets for your first few fish. A spearfishing specialty course will help in this selection. The course will also teach you about local species, laws, and the environment. Take post-class dive trips with the instructor or through the same dive center to gain experience.

Learn Kill Shots

What is the best way to land the fish you shoot? Shoot to "kill" or "stone" the fish you hunt. Shooting fish in a vital spot reduces fish loss and physical effort.

Want to stir up an interesting, if not heated discussion? Ask a group of spearfishermen to describe THE kill shot location. Most agree that

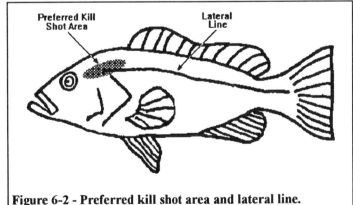

Figure 6-2 - Preferred kill shot area and lateral line.

hitting the area just behind the eye will "stone" a fish and they agree that "windowing" (hitting the fish in the filet meat area) proves embarrassing. For this reason head shots:

- From the side, just behind and level with the eye;
- From above, behind the eye;
- Straight down through the top of the head;

are typically the best kill shots on most fish. A head shot avoids damage to the meaty part of the fish. Even if not a "kill" shot, a spear through the bony, tough head of a fish provides a solid hold for the spearshaft.

Spearfishermen usually disagree when talking about other kill shots. They disagree because most other kill shots are not instant kill shots but rather disabling shots. Hitting a fish in or very near the backbone provides the next best kill shot target. The backbone begins from the fish's head and generally lies along the fish's lateral line to its tail. Even a shot that strikes a fish's tail, if it severs the backbone forward of the caudal (tail) fin, can disable the fish sufficiently to weaken its swimming effort.

Though it generally lies along a fish's lateral line, the location of the backbone varies with fish species. To learn were the backbone lies in the various species, observe its location when cleaning and filleting your fish.

The gill plate provides another effective target area. This bony area provides a good hold for the spearshaft. A shot in the gill plate usually causes profuse bleeding, which quickly weakens the fish. Keep in mind that profuse bleeding may attract predators.

Some fish prove more difficult to "stone" than others. East coast cobia is an example. The cobia's very flat wide head makes a side kill shot almost impossible. A kill shot down through the top of the head often works but the cobia seldom presents itself in a position which allows a top down shot. To disable a cobia, the side shot requires hitting them behind the pectoral fin, high in the lateral line. This does not kill a cobia, but it usually renders its swimming effort ineffective.

Divers who shoot large fish sometimes use barb-less lineshafts. "Why would you want a barb-less spearshaft? Wont the fish get off?" Getting off is exactly what you want a lively large fish to do. A barb-less shaft allows a fish which is not stoned to pull free of the spearshaft easily. This increases safety to the diver by preventing his being dragged around by the fish. It also improves the chances of the fish's survival by leaving a relatively small hole.

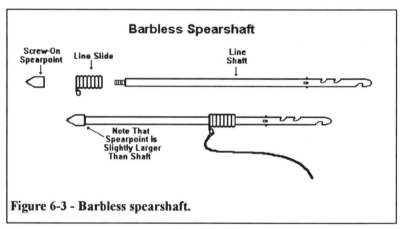

Figure 6-3 - Barbless spearshaft.

To configure a barb-less shaft screw a small spear point, which is slightly wider in diameter than the spearshaft, onto a lineshaft. The spear points used with interchangeable-point spear tips work well for this. This small "flared" point section provides just enough grip once in the fish to keep it from pulling out too easily.

Barb-less spearshafts make stringing and removing stoned fish from the spearshaft easier, also. Improved safety and reduced effort make barb-less spearshafts an attractive alternative for deep water and large fish.

Shooting and stringing
Subduing a stoned fish is fairly straight forward. Stay calm, obtain a secure grip on the fish, and string or bag it quickly. Be prepared, just in case it is only temporarily "killed", to maintain control. When using a stringer, string the fish before removing the spearshaft.

Some freeshaft guns float without a spearshaft loaded into them. Maintain control of the gun and do not let it float to the surface. To free your hands, slide your arm through the bands and let the gun float above you as you deal with the fish. Letting a freeshaft gun float to the surface invites a lost gun. Plus, surfacing to retrieve a floating speargun invites embarrassment. If your gun sinks and you are near the bottom, let the gun lie on the bottom while you string or bag your fish.

"What happens if I spear a fish in a non-vital area?"

Regardless of where you spear a fish, get to it quickly and grasp it firmly by the eye sockets or the meaty "throat" area. Wear gloves. If the fish is near the bottom, pin it by gripping the spearshaft and pushing the tip to the bottom. Avoid pulling the fish to you with the spearshaft. Even when using a line gun, swim to the fish. Pull as little as possible on the line. This reduces the chance of the fish tearing free. Once you get to the fish:

1.   Hold it by gripping it with your hand or pinning it with your forearm or spearshaft;
2.   String it by passing the stringer through its gills or eyes (or by putting it in a game bag);
3.   Remove the spearshaft after the fish is on the stringer or bagged.

When placing a fish in a game bag, insert as much of the fish as possible into the bag head first before removing the spearshaft.

On small fish, the process of subduing and stringing is relatively easy. Medium and large fish or fish which "hole up" in a ledge or wreck require a different approach.

Using your knife, subdue thrashing medium and large fish. (Remember the one mounted so that you can pull it out with either hand?) Dispatch the fish by poking it in a vital area, usually behind the eye. While this may sound gory, it is more humane than allowing a fish to die slowly and it is safer. Some spearfishermen cut the attachment under the gills where the body attaches to the head. This helps control the fish but usually results in severe bleeding and fails to eliminate thrashing.

As discussed in **Chapter 3: Spearguns**, avoid becoming entangled in the line or cable on a line gun or break-away rig.

The best way to retrieve a fish from a ledge or wreck is to pull it out head first by gripping its eye sockets. Avoid tugging on the spearshaft or line. Before retrieving the fish scrutinize the situation. Visibility is often restricted. Wrecks and ledges are usually dark and fish tend to "smoke" the area by finning up silt. Use your flashlight to see where and how the fish is positioned. Check to see how well the spearshaft is holding. If necessary, shoot the fish a second time. Before reaching into any confined area verify that you will not become entangled and that no dangerous marine life shares your fish's hiding place.

Avoid the end of the spearshaft. In their fight to escape, fish, particularly large ones, can turn the blunt end of your own spearshaft into a dangerous lance. Keep one of your gloved hands holding the shaft until you obtain a secure grip on the fish itself. By holding the shaft you can feel when the fish moves and deflect the shaft if it comes your way.

Some fish expertly and securely wedge themselves in a hiding place by flaring their gills. With patience you can usually work them around so that they can be pulled out head first. A push on the spearshaft sometimes causes them to relax their grip. A push can also help press the spearshaft farther through a poorly shot fish. Cutting their gills will weaken a fish quickly but results in severe bleeding. Severe bleeding could attract unwelcome company.

Be aware that fish spines can puncture and sharp gill plates can cut through gloves and exposure suits. Learn how and where to grip various species of fish by practicing on dead ones and by observing experienced fishermen. Avoid allowing fish to brush up against you and stay clear of fish that are thrashing around on deck.

Some fish become buoyant as you ascend. Much like your bcd, some species possess swim bladders that help them maintain neutral buoyancy. Just like air in your bcd, air in fish swim bladders expands and increases buoyancy upon ascent. If you find that your stringer of fish begins to float up, pulling you with it, let it go. You can retrieve it at the surface. Making a slow, safe ascent, much less a safety stop, will be difficult with the stringer of fish pulling you upward. Let it go and collect it at the surface.

Drift diving

Some spearfishing is performed by drift diving or ranging. Advanced or specialty dive courses teach drift diving. It consists of a group of divers drifting with the current, with the boat following above. The boat picks up the divers at the end of the drift. The divers typically use a marker buoy tethered to the surface to help the boat operators keep track of their location. This same technique works well when spearfishing; however, when using a line gun avoid becoming tangled in the drift line.

Ranging resembles drift diving and can use the same buoy technique. By ranging, divers can randomly "hunt" a spearfishing territory without having to return to an anchored boat. A surface buoy, pulled along with them, helps the boat operators follow and pick them up at the end of the dive. This technique allows spearfishermen to cover a broad area without covering the same ground twice.

Deep diving

Spearfishing itself represents an advanced form of diving. Scuba diving deeper than 60 feet also requires advanced diving skill. Spearfishing below 60 feet should only be practiced by divers trained and experienced at both deep diving and spearfishing. Using barb-less shafts will improve safety. Still, no diving should be attempted beyond the recreational safe diving limit of 130 feet. Most recreational dive training organizations recognize this as the limit for recreational diving.

Buddy System

When spearfishermen dive in pairs, they typically swim together, shoulder to shoulder. In this manner each knows the other's location at all times. At other times they agree prior to the dive that one will lead and the other will follow. They usually change leader roles part way through the dive. Either technique works safely. In the leader-follower approach the lead diver should maintain regular contact with the following diver to avoid separation. The following diver should keep his speargun pointed away from the lead diver. The lead diver typically has the advantage of getting first shot at the fish but the following diver often takes fish unseen or missed by the lead diver. The following diver can also help the lead diver subdue a poorly struck fish by shooting it a second time or by helping string the fish.

Sometimes a spearfisherman pairs up with a non-spearfishing buddy. This can be done safely in either the above shoulder to shoulder or leader-follower method. Both divers must accept responsibility for this combination of diving. If the lead diver carries the speargun he must maintain regular contact with the following diver, giving him time to stop and investigate interesting sights. The following diver must keep up and not stop without getting the lead diver's attention. If the following diver carries the speargun, he must keep it pointed safely and not fire if any danger of hitting the other diver exists. The non-spearfishing lead diver should move aside and signal if he spots a target for the spearfishing diver.

Basically the buddy system functions the same when spearfishing as with other types of diving. Divers need to know their buddy's location and assist them if needed. The presence of spearguns simply adds another consideration to the buddy system.

Cleaning your catch

Refer to figure 6-4 through figure 6-7 for a step by step method of producing a boneless fillet from your catch.

Summary

Spearfishing technique develops with experience. Spearfishing skill depends upon coordination, observational skill, shooting accuracy, equipment selection, coordination, and a variety of other subtle skills and senses. Use the information in this chapter to compliment practical experience. As with any sport, practice, practice, practice! Exercise patience. In time you will become an expert spearfisherman.

Figure 6-4 - Begin cleaning by cutting along the top edge of a fish's back, next to the dorsal fin. Continue slicing to separate the filet from the back and other bones.

Figure 6-5 - Once the filet is separated from the backbone, cut behind the gills to free the forward section of the filet from the body of the fish. Leave only the small section of skin and meat at the tail attached.

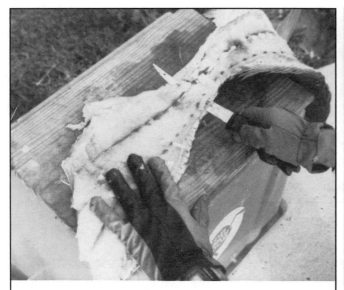

Figure 6-6 - Beginning at the attached tail section, separate the skin from the filet by slicing between the skin and meat for the length of the fillet. Use a sawing motion and rotate the cutting edge of the knife slightly away from the skin.

Figure 6-7 - Finish off by removing the rib bones. Feel for the ends of the ribs with your fingers and make a "V" shaped cut along the bones to remove them.

Review Questions:

1. Why is a check list important when preparing for a dive trip?
2. Why is it important to file a float plan?
3. What is the purpose for marking measurements on your speargun?
4. What do the terms "kill shot" and "stone shot" mean?
5. When stringing a fish, how is a floating gun kept under control?
6. How is a small fighting fish subdued?
7. How are medium and large fish subdued?
8. Before reaching under a ledge to retrieve a "holed up" fish, what precaution should be taken.
9. What effect does a fish's swim bladder have on a diver's buoyancy as the diver surfaces with a stringer of fish?
10. What can be done with a stringer of fish that is causing you to ascend too fast?
11. What is "ranging"?
12. T/F Buddy pairs can either swim shoulder to shoulder or swim with one leading and the other following.

Chapter 7: Spearfishing Safety

Introduction

Spearfishing carries a high degree of responsibility. With any diving activity you assume responsibility for your own safety and for assisting your dive buddy. When spearfishing you must additionally avoid injuring others or, within reason, making them feel uncomfortable. Like diving itself, when performed correctly, adhering to proper safety procedures, spearfishing is very safe.

Objectives
By the end of this section you should be able to:
1. Describe proper speargun handling.
2. List safety considerations in regard to speargun maintenance.
3. List the precautions when handling a speargun.
4. List the precautions when transporting and storing spearguns.
5. Describe five indicators of a properly functioning speargun.
6. Discuss safe and courteous spearfishing practices.
7. Describe a spearshaft caddie.
8. List speargun maintenance procedures.
9. State causes of synthetic material deterioration.
10. List at least five precautions to reduce chance encounters with or injury from dangerous marine life.
11. State how can you help remove a non-spearfisherman's fear about spearguns.

Speargun Safety

Respect spearguns and handle them carefully. Always treat a speargun as you would treat a loaded firearm. The list below summarizes speargun safety practices:

Speargun maintenance
- Make sure spearguns are maintained on a regular basis;
- Before each use verify that they function properly.

Speargun handling
- Always load guns in the water, pointed in a safe direction;
- Never discharge a speargun out of the water;
- Keep the safety on until ready to shoot;
- Before you shoot, make sure that you know what you are shooting at and what is behind it;
- Avoid spearfishing in murky water;
- Never spearfish in crowded areas;
- When passing a gun to someone, always hand it unloaded and butt first, with the speartip facing away from you.

Transportation and storage

- Transport spearguns and spare spearshafts with protective covers over the tips and position them so that they will not damage other equipment or cause injury if the tip cover comes off;
- Store spearguns in a location secured from children.

This may sound like quite a few "rules" but each has a good reason for being on the list. Let's look more closely at them.

Speargun Maintenance

Improperly functioning spearguns are dangerous. On a well maintained gun; 1) The spearshaft locks positively in the catch and trigger mechanism; 2) With line guns the line attaches firmly to the spearshaft and the gun, and the line keeper holds the line securely; 3) The shaft catch notch on the spearshaft shows no sign of wear; 4) On band guns the band material and "wishbone" are in good shape; 5) Barrel, muzzle, and handle components are free from cracks, corrosion, rot, and freeplay; 6) The safety works smoothly and positively; 7) Speartips are sharp, secure, and the barbs function as designed; and, 8) When fired, the trigger mechanism pulls smoothly.

To help keep your gun functioning properly follow the manufacturer's instructions. For general maintenance, wash it with fresh water after each use. Have your gun serviced regularly and before each use perform a speargun safety check. Some checkout procedures require discharging the gun. Discharge spearguns only while submerged and in a safe direction.

1) Positive Shaft Lock

The spearshaft should lock positively in the catch and trigger mechanism. Band powered guns can be checked topside without cocking the bands. Verify that the spearshaft locks firmly in the catch mechanism by loading the spearshaft and pulling in and out firmly on the spearshaft several times. Some freeplay is normal but the spearshaft should hold in the catch and feel securely "locked". Check to verify that the trigger rebounds to its normal position. If it does not, the catch mechanism may not have fully engaged the spearshaft. If the spearshaft does not lock in place or the trigger mechanism does not rebound properly, do not use the gun until it has been serviced. Once you have owned a gun for a period of time, stay alert to changes in the "feel" of the trigger position and operation. This can signal a mechanical problem. Gradual changes in the gun's operation can trick you. Compare your gun's function with that of a new gun of the same model to help assess your gun's condition.

Spring or pneumatically powered guns can only be checked by fully loading, cocking, and test firing them. Perform this test underwater, preferably over sandy bottom to avoid loosing a spearshaft or damaging the speartip.

Note: Some older models of spearguns were prone to discharge accidentally. However, improved spearfishing technology reduces this risk. When purchasing a speargun, select a late model gun from a reputable manufacturer.

2) Line Keeper and Line

With line guns the mechanical line keeper should hold the line securely. If the mechanical line keeper on a line gun does not engage, it signals a potential problem with the entire catch and trigger mechanism. Check this even if you are using the gun with a freeshaft. The line keeper works together with the catch mechanism.

When the trigger is pulled to release the spearshaft the line releases simultaneously. If the line keeper does not engage it indicates that the catch, line, and trigger mechanisms need service.

Also, verify that the line is firmly attached to the spearshaft and the gun. Most lineshafts have a slide to which the line is tied. The other end of the line attaches to the muzzle. Verify that, 1) The line is attached firmly and is free from wear; 2) The slide shows no sign of wear and works smoothly on the spearshaft; and, 3) The slide stop is free of wear. If the line breaks the spearshaft could go beyond the range intended, creating a possible safety problem. Even with the line in good condition do not rely on the line to limit the spearshaft's range. The slide should work smoothly on the spearshaft to prevent jamming.

3) Shaft catch notch

The milled catch notch on the spearshaft should be free from wear. A worn, beveled catch surface prevents the catch mechanism from engaging completely and can result in accidental discharge. Replace suspect spearshafts.

4) Bands

On band powered spearguns the band material and "wishbone" should be in good condition. The bands should be free from rot, which appears as discoloration and small cracks in the band. A band on which the rubber component breaks poses little danger as long as the gun is cocked in the water. Since the band usually breaks during cocking, the result may be a stinging hand. Wearing gloves reduces risk of injury.

As previously mentioned wishbones are the thin metal, monofilament, or nylon components of the band that fit into a spearshaft's band catch notch. When they break it typically occurs when the gun is being cocked. As with the rubber component of the band, a break of a nylon wishbone usually presents no problem as long as the gun is loaded in the water. When a metal wishbone breaks a diver can receive a cut on the palm. Gloves minimize the risk of injury but should not substitute for proper band maintenance.

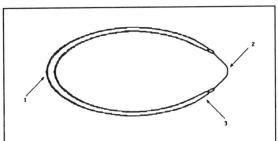

Figure 7-1 - Common break points on bands: 1) Apex; 2) Tie point; 3) Wishbone.

Assessing wishbone fatigue is difficult. With metal material the "V" formed by the wishbone becomes more flexible with fatigue. Monofilament and nylon material fray and show more visible signs of wear with use. Replace "tired" wishbones. The ability to determine when to replace wishbones comes with experience. Since the rubber usually breaks before the wishbone, a safe rule of thumb is to discard the wishbone when the rubber breaks.

5) Muzzle, Barrel, and Handle Integrity

The muzzle, barrel, and handle assemblies on a gun should be solid and free of signs of weakness. Guns with aluminum components should be free from corrosion, particularly at the points where components join. Cracks and signs of swelling at joints indicate corrosion. Even if the components seem to fit together tightly and with no freeplay, the gun is weak and should not be used. With wooden guns the wood should have a healthy wood grain. Dark, discolored, or soggy wood indicates rot. Cracks in the muzzle, barrel, or handle assemblies also indicate weakness.

Freeplay within the joints of any gun is dangerous. Shaft catch mechanisms hold the spearshaft positively when the muzzle, barrel, and handle align rigidly. Flex in this alignment alters the angle of the catch mechanism against the shaft's catch notch. This can result in a dangerous accidental discharge. Regular service minimizes this risk.

When guns with weak muzzle, barrel, and handle assemblies break, it usually occurs when cocking the gun. Also, big fish can pull a weak gun apart. Retire weak and worn spearguns to a place of honor on your wall.

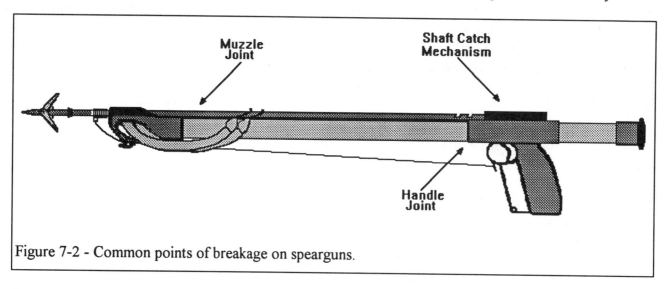

Figure 7-2 - Common points of breakage on spearguns.

6) Safety Mechanism

All mechanical spearguns should have a safety and it should work smoothly. With most band powered guns a topside verification can be conducted. With the spearshaft loaded but with no bands cocked, check the gun's safety by verifying that the:

1. Safety lever moves freely but stays in the position to which it is set;
2. Trigger can not be pulled with the safety on;
3. Shaft releases with the safety off.

Make sure that the spearshaft does not fall out of the gun when performing this test and, as always, point the gun in a safe direction. Some guns have a safety integrated into the trigger mechanism or into the handle. Adapt the above test to suit the type of gun being used.

With spring and pneumatically powered guns the only way to test the functioning of the safety is by loading and discharging ("firing") them underwater. Again, a sandy bottom will reduce the chance of loosing the spearshaft or damaging the speartip when practice firing. While submerged look for tale-tale bubbles that signal a leak in the gun's pressure chamber. To check the safety, first place it in the "safe" position and try to pull the trigger. Next, move the safety to the "fire" position and fire the gun. This verifies that the safety works properly in both positions.

7) Speartip

Speartips should be sharp, securely attached to the spearshaft, and the barbs should function as designed. While not directly related to safety, a sharp and properly functioning speartip is part of a generally well maintained speargun and critical to consistently landing the fish you shoot. When tightening a screw-on speartip, remove the spearshaft from the gun. Then use two pairs of pliers, one to grip the spearshaft, the other the speartip. A dab of thread locking compound helps keep the tip firmly attached. Make a habit of checking the tip's tightness each time you reload. The shock produced from repeatedly discharging the gun will eventually loosen even a tightly threaded tip.

Never tighten a speartip with the spearshaft loaded in a gun. The torque produced by twisting the spearshaft will damage the shaft catch housing and mechanism. Doing so with a loaded and cocked gun is extremely dangerous as the spearshaft will discharge if the spearshaft catch surface rotates off the gun's catch mechanism.

Verify that the barbs open as intended when the spear penetrates its target. For lineshaft tips, verify that the barb hold down ring fits over and holds down the barbs. A smooth working hold down ring simplifies fish removal. Ease of fish removal reduces risk of injury and over exertion. Handle and store spearguns and spare spearshafts so that the point does not accidentally injure anyone or damage other equipment.

Powerheads, devices that use the rapid expansion of gases from an ammunition cartridge, warrant special respect. The following will help keep powerhead use safe:

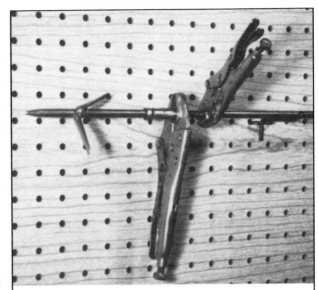

Figure 7-3 - Proper method for tightening speartips.

- Follow the manufacturer's instructions;
- Keep their firing mechanism functioning smoothly;
- Replace springs which are too weak to prevent discharge when fired from the speargun;
- Ensure that the safety pin or clip inserts easily;
- Leave the powerhead's safety in place until ready to fire the powerhead;
- Always load powerheads, with safety pin in place, after entering the water; and, remove the cartridge, again with safety in place, prior to surfacing;
- Handle powerheads with respect. Don't rely on the powerhead's safety;
- Only point powerheads at objects to be shot;
- Never discharge a powerhead against a solid object such as wooden planks, pilings, rocks, or coral;
- Only discharge powerheads in open water, never in air;
- Mount or load speargun mounted powerheads with the gun un-cocked, the powerhead safety pin in, and the speargun safety on;
- Carry powerheads in a pocket reserved only for the powerhead; never in the lapel of a wetsuit;
- Use added caution and common sense when handling powerheads.

Additional information on speartips and powerheads is presented in the **Chapter 5: Special Equipment**.

8) Trigger Pull

When discharging, the trigger should pull smoothly. A smooth trigger pull contributes to accuracy and provides an indication of the mechanical condition of the catch and trigger mechanism. The only way to test trigger pull is by loading, cocking, and discharging the gun. Perform this test while submerged by discharging the spearshaft over a sand bottom, or, more than likely, perform this test in actual use through observation each time you fire the gun.

As part of this test, make sure that the safety works smoothly also. The safety should move from the on position to the off position with only slight resistance. A trigger and safety mechanism that seemed OK when tested topside, without a load on the spearshaft, may bind when under load. If the safety does not function smoothly or the trigger does not pull smoothly, the catch and trigger mechanism need service.

The above guidelines on checking speargun function and mechanical condition will help verify that you are using a mechanically sound gun. Various brands and models of guns may exhibit peculiarities. Adapt your evaluation procedure according to the type and model of gun, following the manufacturer's instructions. Do not use a speargun when in doubt about its condition. Take it to an authorized service center for a check up and maintenance.

Speargun Handling

As stated earlier, treat spearguns like loaded firearms. Loaded or not, firearms should be pointed in a safe direction at all times. The sharp speartip makes this doubly true for spearguns. Pointing a speargun in a safe direction eliminates the possibility of damage or injury from accidental discharge or even from the spearshaft sliding out of an un-cocked gun. Additionally, a speargun's sharp tip can cause injury or damage if it accidentally punches anything. Keep it pointed and stored safely to eliminate this danger.

One approach to speargun safety is to never cock a gun out of the water but always cock and un-cock it underwater. When diving from a boat, enter the water and then have your gun handed to you. The gun should be handed butt first with the point oriented to prevent it from causing injury or damage in the event of a sudden roll of the boat or clumsy hand-off of the gun. The gun should also be un-cocked prior to surfacing and handed into the boat with safety on, butt first, and with the speartip oriented to avoid injury or equipment damage. Avoid securing a gun to a drop line, since the gun is not under control until in a diver's hands.

Only discharge a gun when fully submerged. When discharged underwater, the increased resistance dampens (pun intended) the jolt of the gun's discharge. Guns are not designed to be fired topside. I learned one reason for this the hard way.

A neighbor gave me my first speargun, a small, bright blue, Italian made line gun. It may have been his hand-me-down but to me it was hot stuff! I excitedly hurried home and tried it out by cocking it and discharging it from my back porch toward the pecan tree that stood about twenty feet away. Note the word "toward" The spearshaft didn't make it to the pecan tree. Instead it hit the end of the line, stretched it tight, and recoiled back toward my head with surprising speed. Luckily, I was an agile teenager and quick enough to duck. The screen in the door behind me wasn't so lucky. I don't think I ever explained to Mother how the hole got into that screen.

Keep a gun's safety in the "safe" position until ready to shoot. Since the safety on a well maintained gun functions smoothly, switching it to the "fire" position takes little time during the stalking process. Make the switch when anticipating a potential shot. Keep it in the "safe" position at all other times.

Know your target and what is behind it before shooting. A freeshaft spear can carry approximately fifty feet horizontally in water and farther if discharged well above the bottom. Be aware of where your spearshaft will travel in case it misses or goes completely through its target. With lineshafts or when a freeshaft penetrates partially through a fish, the tip can strike rock, another fish, or cause other damage. Always maintain an awareness of the potential for damage and line up your shot so that there is no incidental damage or injury.

Avoid spearfishing in murky water. This reduces the uncertainty of what is in the line of fire. Some of us would never spearfish if we avoided murky water completely. For safety, if you find yourself spearfishing in less than optimal visibility, always shoot at a downward angle so that the spearshaft strikes the bottom within visible range. Know what is behind your target before you shoot. In particular, know the location of other divers before shooting. Use a line gun in murky water as extra precaution. The line will limit the carry of the spearshaft. Reducing the spearshaft's stopping distance improves safety but do not rely completely upon the line for safety.

Never spearfish in crowed areas. What is a crowed area? Two people spearfishing in an area is a crowd if each does not know the other's position. Also, avoid spearfishing in areas popular to non-spearfishermen. There are plenty of areas to spearfish away from sightseeing areas. The presence of a spearfisherman sometimes makes non-spearfishermen uncomfortable and hurts the reputation of the sport. Besides, the more subtle, less frequented ledge and reef areas typically hold more spearfishing quarry anyway. Let's leave the popular areas to the non-spearfishing divers and avoid mixing spearfishermen and non-spearfishermen on the same dive site. Be careful also when mixing the two on the same dive trip by making sure that spearfishermen handle and store their guns with care and safety.

Transportation

As with firearms, transport spearguns safely. During transportation, secure guns and spearshafts so that they do not fall or move about uncontrollably. As added insurance, cover speartips with protective plastic tips to reduce risk of accidental injury or damage. Speartips can penetrate the plastic covers and covers can come off; so, do not rely on them to avoid injury or damage. Store shafts and guns so that the points can not accidentally injure any one or damage other equipment.

Transport spearshafts in a spearshaft caddie. This provides three benefits; 1) It completely isolates the spearshafts, preventing accidental injury or damage from speartips; 2) It keeps your spearshafts separate from those of other spearfishermen; 3) It makes them easier to carry. A spearshaft caddie can be made from a 2" x 65" length of Schedule 40 PVC pipe with two threaded end caps.

Figure 7-4 - PVC spearshaft caddie.

Care and Storage

Care of spearfishing equipment follows pretty much the same guidelines as that for basic dive gear. Special considerations about spearfishing equipment relates primarily to safety. Proper care and storage include:

- After use, rinse gear with fresh water;
- Allow it to dry thoroughly;
- Inspect it for wear and service it if necessary;
- Store it in a secure, dry, well ventilated, dark location.

Most water in which we dive contains dissolved salts and other minerals. Using fresh water, thoroughly flush all dirt, salt, and minerals from dive gear. A soak in mild dish soap will help remove stubborn salt deposits in hard to reach places such as the trigger mechanism. When it evaporates salt water leaves behind abrasive and hydroscopic salt crystals. Salt is hydroscopic, meaning that it draws moisture to itself. This explains why un-rinsed gear continues to feel slightly damp after it has "dried". Salt crystals cause fiber breakdown, even cuts, in fabrics in which they become imbedded. As for its effect on metals, the chemical nature of salt accelerates oxidation (rust and corrosion) in metals.

In addition to the usual "contaminants", found in dive site water, spearfishing exposes dive equipment to "fish ooze". This consists of fish oil, blood, and other contaminants. Fish ooze can be caustic and exudes a bad odor; in other words, it stinks. Spearfishermen occasionally catch lobster. Lobster ooze, if not quickly washed from surfaces, sets to an almost plastic resin hardness. This makes it extremely difficult to remove. Wash your gear thoroughly with fresh or mild soapy water as soon as possible.

Once rinsed, hang spearfishing gear along with the rest of your gear to drain and dry. Water that drips from dive gear takes with it some of the remaining salt and other contaminants. Spare bathroom showers make ideal drying areas. They are out of direct sunlight, provide good drainage, and can be secured from children.

Before storing your gear, inspect it for signs of wear. Replace worn line and rotten power bands, sharpen and tighten speartips, mend torn game bags, and repair or take in for service any questionable component. Performing maintenance after each use helps ensure that your gear will be ready the next time you need it. You will still need to inspect it prior to your next dive but pre-storage maintenance will prevent most disappointing surprises when you get a last minute call to go spearfishing.

Store gear in a cool, dark location with good ventilation, and away from automobile exhausts and electric motors. Why?

- Cool temperature slows the chemical processes which causes corrosion and deterioration;
- Sunlight is the number one enemy to synthetic materials;
- Ventilation reduces corrosion and mildew enhancing moisture;
- Automobile exhaust includes a variety of caustic chemicals and electric motors give off oxygen rich ozone. These air borne "contaminants" accelerate corrosion and deterioration.

Remember to choose a storage location inaccessible to children. A locked storage cabinet or gymnasium style locker works well for this. Additionally, remove the spearshafts and power bands from guns, just in case one accidentally gets into the wrong hands. Segregating the components reduces the chance of the gun causing accidental injury or damage. Store dry spearshafts in a spearshaft caddie.

Before storing equipment, apply a light coating of silicone preservative to the non-rubber components. This helps protect and lubricate equipment. Silicone lubricant on the gun's mechanical and metal parts and the spearshaft reduces corrosion. (Even stainless steel corrodes!)

Avoid using silicone or petroleum based sprays and oils on synthetic speargun components or mechanisms. Some speargun parts, such as power bands and safety friction washers, are constructed of silicone or latex rubber. Lubricants accelerate deterioration of these components, shortening their useful life.

One of the best methods for extending the life of speargun power bands is to seal them in a plastic "zipper" bag and store them in your freezer. This reduces and almost eliminates rot between uses. Be sure to thaw them slowly. Take care not to flex frozen bands and don't accidentally throw them on the grill with the hot dogs on your next cookout! Burning rubber smells awful.

Dangerous Marine Life
"What about sharks!?"

When divers talk of safety and spearfishing the issue of sharks usually arises. Sharks, barracuda, moray eels, jellyfish, and other dangerous sea life are considerations in any diving activity. Seldom are divers, spearfishermen included, attacked while diving. The few instances that occur usually result from divers reaching into holes, feeding fish, or harassing sharks. While there are various forms of dangerous marine life, the following addresses the most common concerns related to hunting underwater.

Eels

Moray eels are the most well recognized of the perceived dangerous eels but wolf and conger eels deserve respect also. Eels can inflict serious and infectious bite wounds but seldom come out of their holes. They usually stay hidden in crevices during daytime. They have bitten divers, usually divers who were feeding them or reaching into crevices after lobster or speared fish. Avoiding these practices significantly reduces your chance of being bitten by an eel. Lesson: "Leave them alone, and they will leave you alone."

Barracuda

Barracuda, sometimes called "wolves of the sea", have sharp teeth set in menacing looking large jaws. Despite this colorful label, barracuda seldom bite divers. There are accounts of them biting divers and swimmers but barracuda tend to move away when divers approach. However, they occasionally take fish from a diver's spear. If this happens, let the barracuda have your fish. Better to lose a fish than be bitten, even if by accident, by a barracuda. Also, avoid shooting or feeding barracuda. Some divers avoid shooting other fish in their presence. Lesson: Like with eels, "You leave them alone, and they will leave you alone."

Sharks

Shark attacks are also rare with divers, including spearfishermen. Most shark attacks seem to be either accidents of mistaken identity or the result of a diver molesting a shark. Some notorious attacks on underwater hunters are attributed to sharks biting California abalone divers. Some experts feel that this type of attack results from the diver's resemblance to the seals and sea lions upon which the sharks usually feed. Lesson: "Don't look like a seal!"

Some attacks have occurred from divers molesting sharks. Never pull a shark's tail. Even nurse sharks, which often lie lethargically under ledges, can turn around quickly and leave a serious bite injury and broken bones. Lesson: "Let sleeping sharks lie."

In some areas, sharks are known for taking fish from the spears of divers. Most of these incidents do not result in injury to the diver. Be aware that it can happen and refrain from spearing fish when sharks are present. Lesson: "When being mugged, give them your money."

Some sharks are simply dangerous. The great white shark is the most notorious of the dangerous sharks but other species such as gray reef, hammerhead, mako, bull, dusky, tiger, and blue sharks share a dangerous reputation. Fortunately, these sharks are rare and more common in deep water. Lesson: "Stay out of bad neighborhoods and away from dangerous characters."

Other Dangerous Marine Life

Sharks, barracuda, and eels receive the most attention, regarding dangerous marine life. However, other fish, such as grouper and triggerfish, also create occasional problems. Large aggressive grouper, such as jewfish, sometimes take fish away from divers. Their canine like teeth can leave a nasty gash. Triggerfish, when excited by the prospect of a free meal, sometimes accidentally bite divers. While not fatal, their painful bite can break the skin or leave a pretty nasty "hickey" of a blood blister. Lesson: "Avoid tempting any aggressive sea life with speared fish."

(If you shoot triggerfish, which are tasty fish, string them though the gills and mouth. This will prevent them from biting you.)

Spearfishing Marine Life Safety

Safety practices to help keep you safe from injury by marine life include:

- Always swim calmly and observe your surroundings. Remain alert for dangerous marine life or conditions (clear water and calm seas help when looking for dangerous marine life);
- Promptly remove speared fish from the water;
- Do not carry speared fish with you;
- Do not shoot fish when sharks or barracuda are present;
- Calmly get out of the water if you feel threatened by a shark or other marine life; (Remember, sharks and barracuda can out swim even the fastest swimmer so retreat calmly and remain facing them. Also, stay near the bottom if possible.)
- Avoid touching the bottom where urchins, fire coral, and abrasive rock can cause a painful flesh wound;
- Never reach into a crevice or under a ledge;
- If a barracuda, shark, or jewfish takes a fish you have speared, let them keep it. Neither fish nor spearshaft is worth getting injured over;
- Do not dive in areas being fished by fishermen using chum;
- Consider carrying a powerhead;
- Do not shoot barracuda, sharks, or other potentially dangerous marine life;
- Do not dive in areas known for dangerous marine life;
- Do not feed marine life;
- Do not harass marine life;
- If you feel uncomfortable during a dive, trust your sixth sense and calmly get out of the water.

One reason for that "uncomfortable feeling" might relate to the old war movies about bombers. When the enemy fighter airplanes disappeared, look out.... The antiaircraft guns were about to open fire. It can be the similar in diving. If one minute the fish are all around you, the next they are either gone, hugging the rocks, or behaving differently. It is time to take a good look around!

Fortunately, injuries from marine life rarely occur. If they do happen they are usually minor. With any injury from marine life, use good judgment and seek medical attention when necessary. For advice on any diving related injury, contact the Divers Alert Network (DAN) at Duke University Medical Center in North Carolina:

Non-emergency diving questions: (919)684-2948
Diving emergencies: (919)684-8111
Membership information (800)446-2671
Internet address: http://www.dan.ycg.org.

DAN
Duke University Medical Center
PO Box 3823
Durham, NC 27710

Summary

Most spearfishing equipment safety relates to your parents' common sense advice not to run with scissors or cut toward yourself with a knife. Now you have graduated to spearguns, which are powerful, have sharp ends, and a long trajectory. By learning and following spearfishing safety practices you will contribute to keeping spearfishing respectable, enjoyable, and rewarding.

As a spearfisherman, you will at times find yourself around non-spearfishermen. One of the first reactions that I have observed in people, who are not familiar with spearguns, is anxiety that guns are always cocked and could go off at any minute. Take a moment to remove their "mystery induced" anxiety by safely showing them a little bit about your speargun and how it works. Also explain spearfishing to them.

Spearfishing provides a positive, environmentally friendly means of harvesting from the sea. It results in the least by-catch (waste caused by taking undersized fish) of any fish harvesting method, leaves behind no "dangerous litter" and is governed by the same bag limits as other means of fish harvest. Some people do not realize this until it is explained. **Appendix B: Ethics, Environment, and Law** provides additional background for favorably presenting spearfishing.

Safety around sea life requires common sense also. Avoid diving practices that increase the possibility of injury from marine life. Remember, you are in their element. Learn to recognize dangerous marine animals and their behavior. Treat them with respect.

Remain alert to the safety practices of other divers and spearfishermen. Some divers learned to spearfish by buying a speargun and teaching themselves. They may not understand spearfishing safety. Speak up when you feel that another diver is acting dangerously. Whether the other diver is or is not aware of the danger of his actions, emphasize your right to safety.

By demonstrating your knowledge of spearfishing, a concern for safety, and your respect for the environment you will help keep spearfishing a safe and vital diving specialty.

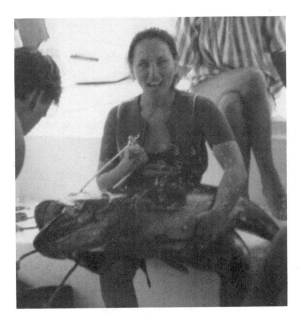 

Review Questions:

1. In general, how is a speargun handled?
2. List the safety considerations in terms of speargun maintenance.
3. List the precautions when handling a speargun.
4. List the precautions when transporting and storing spearguns.
5. Describe five indicators of a properly functioning speargun.
6. T/F Murky water is safer for spearfishing than clear water.
7. T/F Spearfishermen, as a matter of etiquette, should leave the scenic dive sites to sightseeing divers.
8. When should a gun be cocked?
9. Why should spearguns not be fired out of water?
10. When should a gun's safety be switched to the "fire" position?
11. What is a spearshaft caddie?
12. What maintenance and storage procedures should be followed for spearguns?
13. What is the number one cause of deterioration in synthetic materials?
14. List five precautions to reduce chance encounters with or injury from dangerous marine life when spearfishing?
15. How can you help remove a non-spearfisherman's fear about spearguns?

Chapter 8: After the Spearfishing Course

Introduction

What do you do after you complete your spearfishing specialty course? If you own a boat where do you go? If you do not have your own boat, with whom do you dive? What organized activities are there for spearfishing?

Knowing how to actually spear and bring a fish back to the boat is only part of the art of spearfishing. Knowing were to go and with whom to go is just as important. This chapter presents information on dive spot location, spearfishing dive boat etiquette, dive clubs, and spearfishing tournaments.

Objectives
By the end of this section you should be able to:
1. List several sources for locating dive sites.
2. Explain how to find your own "secret" spots.
3. State the main rule when diving from someone else's boat.
4. List some of the services provided by dive clubs.
5. Explain the benefits in attending or participating in spearfishing tournaments.

Dive site location

Possessing spearfishing skill meets only part of the talent and knowledge necessary for bringing fresh fish to your table. Knowing where to find the fish sometimes poses a greater challenge. Spearfishing specialty courses usually include information about spearfishing sites and the legalities involved in where you can spearfish in your area. Organized dive trips handle the concerns about spearfishing location. But, where do you dive when you are ready to spearfish on your own?

Fishermen traditionally keep their fishing spots secret. After all, if they give you their spots they would no longer be secret. Spearfishermen protect the secrecy of their dive sites too. They may give you some "not so secret" spots but will hang onto the better ones. However, there are ways to find places to spearfish.

Books, charts, and lists of fishing locations are available for most areas that provide a good list of local fishing and diving locations. Such publications can be found at book stores, dive centers, and fishing tackle supply stores. Even though these "published" fishing and dive site locations contain no secret locations, they do provide excellent seed lists from which to build your own private list.

Usually, where one natural ledge or rock pile is found others can be found in the same area. Use a computer program such a The LORAN/GPS Program from Andren Software (see bibliography) to help predict where to look. Search for distribution patterns in the alignment of the ledges and reefs. Use a good loran or GPS unit along with a good depth recorder to search for new sites near already known fishing spots. In shallow water, tow snorkelers on sleds to look for ledges, wrecks, and other dive sites. (Remember, never use scuba while towing on a sled. The risk is too great. See **Chapter 5: Special Equipment** for additional information on using sleds.)

Even well known fishing spots deserve an occasional try. A bit of reverse psychology sometimes applies to published fishing spots. Fishermen think that everybody else has already fished them and pass them by. Also, some species of fish are transient or semi-transient. Sites that receive heavy pressure continue to produce from one day to the next as new fish move in.

A sample of dive site publications include; 1) *Coastal Loran Coordinates, Texas to Maine* (Stebbins and Stebbins, 1990); 2) *Coastal Loran Coordinates, Great Lakes* (Stebbins and Stebbins, 1990); 3) *Coastal Loran Coordinates, Pacific* (Stebbins and Stebbins, 1990); 4) *Fish & Dive Florida and The Keys* (O'Keefe and Larsen, 1992); 4) *Diving Guide to Underwater Florida* (DeLoach, 1993); 5) *Southern California's Best Beach Dives* (Sheckler and Sheckler); 6) *International Sailing Supply Fish and Dive Charts* (International Sailing Supply, 1991). See the Bibliography for additional information on these publications.

Talk with experienced spearfishermen in your area to learn the location of popular or commonly known spots. Do not expect to learn the location of their secret spots. They probably will not give them to you. And, if you are invited to spearfish with an experienced diver, do not "steal" their secret spots. Divers who do this find themselves receiving few repeat invitations. When in doubt, tactfully ask if the spot is a known number and whether the other person minds if you come back to it.

Boat Diving Etiquette

A good approach to gain additional experience and learn more about the area that you plan to spearfish is to dive with other spearfishermen. When you receive an invitation to dive with someone else, what can you do to encourage a repeat invitation?

The main rule when you ride on someone else's boat is to be considerate. What does being considerate mean? The following guidelines will help make you a welcome guest aboard a boat:

- Take a safe boating course from the US Power Squadron or US Coast Guard Auxiliary. (See also *Piloting, Seamanship, and Small Boat Handling* in the Bibliography.)
- Make yourself useful. Ask how you can help and for instructions on how to perform tasks with which you are unfamiliar. A guest who enthusiastically helps with hauling anchor makes themselves especially popular.
- Clean up spills or fish ooze immediately and help clean the boat when you return to port.
- Wear non-marring deck shoes.
- Avoid dropping weights or tanks on deck or punching holes in your host's bimini top or upholstery with your speartip.
- Be careful moving around on board to avoid hurting others or yourself. Don't be a klutz. Think before acting. Maintain a handhold to help maintain your balance and sit or stand out of the way of others as much as possible.
- Smoke only if the captain does.
- Bring only what you will need and pack compactly in soft-sided bags and containers.
- Ask what you should bring in the way of food, drinks, and ice chests.
- Obtain a dive briefing from the captain or dive leader as to which way to swim from the anchor to find the dive site, what to expect, how long to dive, and what constitutes a recall signal. (Boat engines can be heard by divers if revved up in gear. Three evenly spaced one second bursts of the engine make an effective recall signal. The operator should verify that there are no divers near the boat when performing this signal.) Remember, if there are no fish on a site, a spearfishing

dive will be shorter in duration than a leisure dive. Get back on board and situated quickly so that the captain can move to the next spot.

- When diving from an anchored boat, swim down the anchor line and verify that the anchor holds securely. If not, surface and inform the captain or crew.
- On board, keep your gear neatly stowed and organized.
- Help with expenses. The US Coast Guard has relaxed its definition of a vessel carrying passengers for hire so that boating expenses can now be shared. Ask the captain what amount is appropriate. Operating a boat includes many expense items in addition to fuel and oil.

Dive Clubs

Dive clubs provide another good source for spearfishing information and experience. Investigate clubs in your area to identify ones which orient toward spearfishing. Visit several clubs then join one that suits your style and skill level. Dive club listings are available from the Underwater Society of America, Florida Skin Divers Association, New York State Divers Association, and similar groups. (See appendix.) Regional dive publications, such as Florida Scuba News, contain dive club listings as well. Many dive centers support "in store" dive clubs.

Computer online services sometimes provide dive club information. Check the following dive related online information sources:

- America Online's Scuba Forum
- CompuServe's Scuba Forum
- Florida Scuba News web page at: http://www.emi.net/gulfstream/fsn/fsnhead.html
- Rodale's Scuba Diving magazine's web page at: http://www.scubadiving.com
- Scuba Times magazine's web page at: http://www.scubatimes.com

This represents only a sample of dive related information sources available online. You can find more by searching the Internet.

Clubs organize outings, social events, as well as various types of dive trips. Some clubs involve their members in shaping regulations that affect diving, environmental clean-up, and community issues. Your participation in spearfishing and non-spearfishing club activities with a dive club will contribute to your overall experience as a diver and as a diving citizen. After joining a club, continue to dive with experienced spearfishermen outside the club as well. You may be able to import ideas and techniques new to the club.

Spearfishing Tournaments

Competing in spearfishing tournaments will accelerate your spearfishing learning process. Spearfishing tournaments bring out some of the best spearfishermen. Even if you do not compete, just by being around a tournament and observing you will pick up tidbits of useful information.

Tournaments typically consist of the following events:

- Registration is usually conducted either the night before or the morning of the tournament. Some tournaments offer advance registration. Registration sometimes requires a registration fee for either an individual, a team, or both, depending upon the tournament's organization.

- Captain and competitor's briefings are usually held the night before or the morning of the event. For multi-day events organizers sometimes hold briefings at the beginning of each tournament day. Briefings include information on last minute rule changes, boundary clarification, finish line definition, and establishing the official time.

- Tournament competition typically extends between set starting and ending times. Some tournaments require that boats stay within a certain depth limit. "Open" tournaments typically impose no depth limit; however, divers should dive within their limits and recreational diving guidelines.

- Fish weigh-in starts about one hour prior to the finish time for the tournament. Most tournaments provide a time keeper who monitors the weigh-in line to ensure that all contestants report to the weigh-in, with their fish iced down in containers, before the finish time. Some tournaments establish a finish line. Anyone arriving late is disqualified.

  Weigh-in is an exciting event where fish are measured and weighed to the sound of cheers from teams whose fish finish high and groans as a team's fish are replaced on the leader board. At the weigh-in, notice the manner in which fish are handled; notice where they were shot. Listen in on conversations of the better competitors. At most tournaments you will get an opportunity to see spearfishing gear and the boats used for spearfishing. Again, observe and learn. If you see something of interest, ask about it. Most spearfishermen feel a sense of pride in their special configurations and will readily explain how they work.

- Award ceremonies are held either the day of the tournament or the following day. Top spearfishermen in each fish category receive special recognition. Some tournaments recognize overall individual and team winners. Fish weight or a point system determines finish position. Some tournaments award prizes by allowing competitors to pick from a table of prizes, depending upon their finish position in the tournament.

When participating in a tournament for the first time, try to go with a tournament experienced diver or team of divers. Time constraints force a fast pace on tournament diving. Divers usually drop off on dive sites for several drift or ranging style dives during the course of a tournament day. Each buddy pair alternately dives, then operates the boat. For this reason a team usually scouts an area several days prior to a major tournament to locate several "spots". This provides a good opportunity for the team members to become accustomed to each other and learn to operate the boat.

Due to the challenge of competition, tournaments hone a spearfisherman's skill. Give tournament competition a try either as a competitor or spectator. One way to break in with a team is to volunteer to drive the boat or serve as a "bubble watcher" rather than participate as a spearfisherman. This will give you a chance to observe and gain experience before actually getting into the competition yourself.

The following rule list and announcement describes a typical spearfishing tournament.

Sample Open Spearfishing Tournament Rules

A. Trophies will be awarded for the largest fish/lobster in each category.

B. One prize pick per diver, except holders of drawn tickets and special awards.

C. Prize winners will be judged on largest remaining fish in each category, after previous winners entries are deleted. Prize pick order by species with size restrictions:

1.	Grouper/Scamp	21" min. all grouper and scamp.
2.	Snapper	20" min. red snapper, 14" all others
3.	Hogfish	14" min. size, fork
4.	Spiny/shovel lobster	3" on carapace spiny lobster, must not be speared.
5.	Jack/Cobia/Cuda	36" min. jacks and cuda, 33" min. cobia fork
6.	Sheepshead/Triggerfish	14" min. fork

D. Mystery ticket drawing starts in seventh position (nineteenth pick overall) at the end of the third round. Mystery tickets will given for each fish turned in and limited to five per fish category, per contestant. In addition to mystery tickets, one ticket will be given in each sponsored fish category when a fish is turned in of that category's species. Fish Category final drawings will be held at the end of final prize table selection for each sponsored category.

E. All State and Federal rules, size limits, license requirements, and bag limits apply.

F. Decisions and interpretations of these rules by the tournament director and his designees shall be final.

G. Both tank and free diving are permissible. There is no restriction on the number of tanks allowed. In order to be eligible, fish must have been caught by the contestant using a spear loaded or propelled by his/her own muscle power. Lobster may be grabbed or netted as allowed by lobster regulations.

H. Scales will be open for weighing fish at 4:30 p.m. Contestants not in line with their gutted and properly iced down fish by 7:30 p.m. will be disqualified. Fish must be brought to the weigh-in line on ice in a container.

I. There are no boundaries. Bay diving is permitted.

J. No boat may approach under power within 150 feet of an anchored boat flying a diver's and/or alpha flag.

K. No powerheads allowed.

L. Each contestant is requested to wear an inflatable rescue device.

M. No contestant may receive assistance with any fish until he/she has one hand on the boat. Contestants may help each other net or grab lobster.

N. Fish must be checked in at the weigh-in area by contestants from the same boat.

O. In the event that a boat becomes disabled, all contestants' catch and briefing bracelets may be brought into designated weigh-in area by any contestant from disabled boat. All rules, including check-in procedures apply.

P. All fish and lobster weighed from any one contestant must be weighed at one time. All fish and lobster brought to the weigh-in area will be considered fish and lobster to be weighed and property of the sponsoring organization. Any exceptions will be cause for disqualification.

Q. All contestants must be present at the sign up and divers' meeting to receive their briefing bracelets.

Invitation to Participate
30th Annual Spearfishing Open
Worlds Largest and Best Spearfishing Tournament!

Hosted by the **Spearfishing Underwater Club**
August 25, 26, 27 at the beautiful Super Resort

Once again the Spearfishing Club proudly presents the prestigious Spearfishing Open Tournament. This year roughly 250 of the best divers in the United States will compete for over $25,000 in prizes. Several past champions will be there. This is truly an event for the area to take pride in.

If you have not been to the Spearfishing Open in previous years, we invite you to join us for the spectacle, camaraderie, and even if you are not a former champion, the prizes! Just about every one wins, and most win much more than they expected. If you don't dive, at least visit the weigh-in on Saturday August 26, beginning at 4:30 p.m. in the Resort parking lot. Absolutely no fishing tournament of any kind in the world can match the diversity of species on display. For example some of the past records include:

Grouper - North American Catch Record 111.5 lbs. - Gary Zumwalt, 1991
Hogfish - 20.4 lbs. - Steve Townsend, 1990
Sheepshead - 9.3 lbs. - Ray Hinton, 1980
Amberjack - 85 lbs. - David Fair, 1994
Snapper - 54 lbs. - Dick Newman, 1981
Lobster - 12.3 lbs. - Scott Wilner, 1992

Event Schedule

Friday, August 25: 6 p.m. to 9:30 p.m.
Registration and Party @ the Super Resort, 10650 Super Location Blvd., Somewhere Near Water, USA, Entry fee: $30 per contestant.
9:00 p.m. Competitor and captain's meeting and ticket issue. Start of tournament.

Saturday, August 26, 4:30 p.m.
Weigh-in begins at the Resort. 7:30 p.m. Tournament finish - all participants must be checked in with their fish IN THE WEIGH-IN LINE. Weigh-in continues until all fish are weighed or until there are no responses to the weigh-master's last call for fish. The public is welcome at NO CHARGE for this event.

Sunday, August 27, 11:00 a.m., until approximately 2:00 p.m.
Award presentation and prize selection. A random drawing for a major prize will be the final event.

Summary

Becoming a skilled spearfisherman requires knowledge and practice. Gain as much knowledge as you can from experienced spearfishermen. You will learn from everyone with whom you dive. (Though you may learn what not to do from some of them.) When invited on a dive, show consideration to your host and other divers. Avoid trying to impress other divers. Ask questions when something is unfamiliar. Relax and enjoy the process of learning to spearfish.

Happy spearfishing!

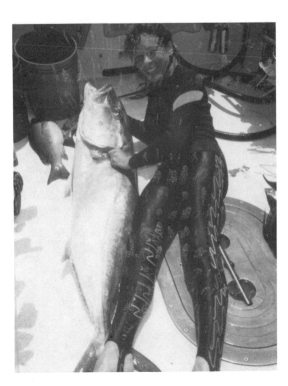

Review Questions:
1. What sources can be used to locate dive sites?
2. How can you find your own "secret" spots?
3. What is the main rule when diving from someone else's boat?
4. What services do dive clubs provide?
5. What benefit is there in attending or participating in spearfishing tournaments?

Appendix A: Specialty Underwater Hunting

Underwater hunting encompasses a variety of activities. Most divers associate hunting with some form of game taking activity such as spearfishing, lobstering, or abalone diving. However, such activities as shell collecting, stalking with a camera, bottle collecting, wreck hunting, treasure hunting, prospecting, and any other activity involving searching also fall within underwater hunting's scope.

Specialty Underwater Hunting addresses various types of underwater searching, catching, and collecting. This section of Specialty Underwater Hunting represents the initial installment of a planned continuing forum on underwater hunting topics. These first two topics cover lobstering and scalloping as practiced in Florida. Topics of interest in other regions and updates on spearfishing itself will be available in the future. This will allow you to develop an underwater hunter reference library. Send in the post card in the back of this book to receive notices of upcoming articles. (Your name and address will only be used by Active Adventure and not released to the junk mail generators.)

Specialty Underwater Hunting -- Lobstering

Introduction

In the search for delectable goodies from the sea few treats top the taste of lobster. While the species of pincher-less lobster on the United States East and West (Pacific) Coasts differ slightly, divers treasure these tasty prizes on both coasts. Divers in the Pacific must catch lobster by hand. Atlantic and Gulf of Mexico divers can use nets and snares. This installment focuses on hunting Florida Spiny Lobster.

"Catching" Lobster

As nocturnal feeders, Florida spiny lobster make their daytime homes in rock piles, ledges, and wrecks. Their antenna often protrude from their hiding place, giving away their location. Though their antenna make a tempting handle by which to grab them, doing so will result only in a hand full of broken, lobster-less antenna.

In United States waters divers usually tickle spiny lobster out of their lair with a plastic or aluminum "tickle stick" and guide them into a small landing or "catch" net. It is important to guide the lobster, tail first, into the net rather than trying to move the net to the lobster. Moving the net will spook them.

After the lobster enters the net, press the hoop of the net flat, open side down, against the ocean bottom. Then grab the lobster with gloved hands to keep it from "bouncing" its way out of the net.

Tickle sticks come in a variety of styles and colors. Aluminum tickle sticks typically include a slight bend in the end. Some divers feel this helps in getting the stick behind the lobster. Stick color is of less importance than stiffness. A stiff stick helps with coaching

Figure A-1 - Tournament winning "bug".

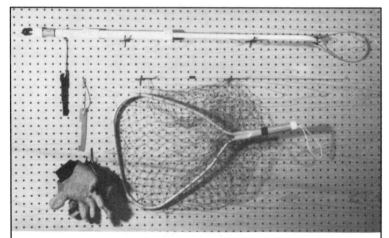

Figure A-2 - Lobstering tools (bottom to top): Gloves, catch net, tickle stick and guage, lobster snare.

stubborn lobster out of their hiding places. A long stick provides an advantage with lobster in deep crevices.

The catch net should be relatively small and made of polypropylene mesh. It seems easier to coach a lobster into a clear or green net than into a black net. They do not seem quite as afraid of blue nets as they are black.

Avoid cotton mesh nets. Cotton mesh fouls easily in gear and bottom snags. Cotton mesh also makes removing the lobster from the net difficult and time consuming.

One style of net comes with a small plastic end cap with a shock cord loop protruding from the end of the net's handle. The loop helps in carrying the net, but the cap can easily pull off, resulting in a lost net. To avoid this, remove the cap before using the net to remove the temptation of carrying the net by the loop.

Freediving and scuba are permitted when taking lobster in the United States. In Florida you must possess a current salt water fishing license and lobster stamp in order to legally take lobster. In the Bahamas, lobster may be speared with a pole spear or Hawaiian sling but must be taken only by freediving. Check your local laws and regulations for special regulations in your area.

Besides using a tickle stick and net, snares also work well for taking lobster. Lobster snares are easier to carry as additional equipment while spearfishing than a net and tickle stick. Available from various manufacturers, snares come in a variety of designs. The basic design of snare incorporates thin PVC tubing through which heavy monofilament line or plastic coated wire cable is threaded. The line or cable is formed into a sliding noose at one end of the tubing. A smaller loop is formed at the other end for use as a pull ring for tightening the noose. The lobster is captured by coaching its tail into the noose and closing the noose tightly. Tickle sticks are sometimes used along with snares to position the lobster in the noose.

Some snares allow one handed operation by combining the snare with an automatic noose tightener. Automatic snares are "cocked" by pulling them out against the tension of a section of surgical tubing and locked into place by a friction catch. Once around a lobster's tail, the diver closes the noose by releasing the catch with a thumb or finger.

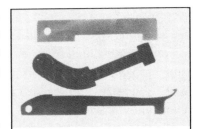

Figure A-3 - Lobster gauges. Photo courtesy of Sport Diver Mfg.

Several lobster may occupy one hiding place. Look closely. The bigger lobster typically stay farther back and push the smaller ones forward. Since the size of the antennae can deceive you it is difficult to tell which lobster are "keepers". To get a good look at the lobster in the back of the crevasse, tickle out and chase away the smaller lobster, taking care not to injure them. A small flashlight comes in handy for looking into crevices.

Slipper or bulldozer lobster are other types of lobster common to the South Atlantic and Gulf of Mexico. They are smaller than spiny lobster but every bit as flavorful, if not better tasting. Like spiny lobster, slippers also hide under ledges and often attach to ledge roofs. A light helps in finding this species. At first glance they resemble a bump in the natural rock of the ledge and in dim light are difficult to distinguish. Slower than spiny lobster, they can be scooped up with a small net or, if there are no dangerous companions under the ledge with them, grabbed by hand.

Figure A-4 - Slipper lobster.

Once caught, measure and check each lobster for eggs before putting it into a catch bag. There is no size limit for slipper lobster. Florida spiny lobster, however, must measure over three inches on their carapace. Each diver must carry a lobster gauge, which consists of a flat piece of plastic or aluminum with a three inch cutout. Measure from the ridge between a lobster's eye horns to the back edge of the carapace. If the edges of the gauge's cutout slip over the solid part of the carapace, the lobster is too short. Small lobster are referred to as "shorts". Release shorts un-harmed.

Most divers carry lobster gauges attached to their tickle sticks. Others carry them tied to the zipper of their dive skin, a "D" ring on their bcd, the drawstring on their swim trunks, or other convenient location. Tickle stick carried gauges tend to tangle in the catch net, especially if the gauge is attached with a key ring loop. This can waste precious time while untangling it. If you carry a gauge attached to your personal gear you always have a gauge with you. Either end of a gauge-less tickle stick can be used to coach a lobster out of its hiding place with no time wasted turning the stick around or untangling it.

Egg bearing females are illegal to take and should be left un-injured even if they are of legal size. Female lobster carry eggs in a spongy mass under their tails. Due to their importance in sustaining the lobster population, completely avoid molesting egg bearing lobster.

When catching lobster, avoid injuring them or breaking off their legs or antenna. Undersized lobster must be released. Others simply escape. While lobster can re-grow legs and antenna, they are handicapped, reducing their chance of survival. Additionally, this stunts their growth through their next several molts. (Lobster grow by shedding their hard outer shells; a process called molting. Soft lobster have just undergone a molt. They are legal to take as long as they meet the over three inch size requirement.)

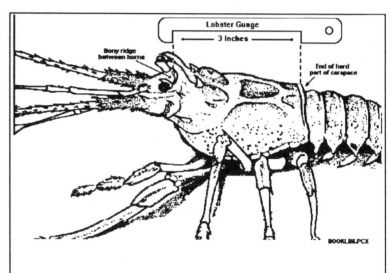

Figure A-5 - Measuring a lobster's carapace. Courtesy of the St. Petersburg Underwater Club.

Catch bags with heavy gauge wire or plastic hoop closures (Figure 5-21) are durable and work well for "bagging" lobster. Avoid bags with small coiled spring closure latches. These locks tend to tangle in the mesh of lobster nets. Also, bags with plastic spring loaded closure lids, while they make bagging lobster easy, tend to be weak and bulky. A solid nylon bag or a bag with a nylon upper part and mesh lower part works well as the slippery nylon simplifies pushing already caught lobster to the bottom of the bag. This helps prevent their escape when bagging the next. With the half nylon and half mesh type of bag, lobster like to hide in the dark nylon section after being "bagged". To prevent this push them to the bottom of the bag as you catch them, then keep them there by putting a half twist in the middle of the bag. This can be done with any type bag to ready it for receiving the next catch.

Some bags include a bottom closure to help simplify removing the lobster. Be sure to secure the bottom closure before bagging your lobster, otherwise they will escape.

Preparing Lobster for the Table

Clean lobster by wringing their tails from their heads (carapaces). Using a knife to first slice away the connecting tissue helps keep more meat attached to the tail. Before discarding the head, save an antenna or two for use in cleaning out the part of intestine that runs the length of the tail.

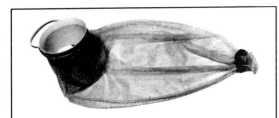

Figure A-6 - Bottom closure bag with spring lid. Courtesy Sport Diver Mfg.

Remove the tail intestine by inserting a small section of antenna, spines facing backward into the orifice at the base of the tail then pulling it back out. The spines will hook and remove the intestine. For stubborn cases, insert the tool farther into the tail. It sometimes pushes the intestine out instead of hooking it.

Be sure to wash and scrub away lobster ooze from the boat, ice chest, dive gear, and cleaning area. As it dries lobster ooze hardens to almost the consistency of cured fiberglass resin. Wash it off before it dries.

Two methods work well for storing lobster: 1) Freeze them in fresh water; 2) Double wrap them in plastic wrap then place them in a zipper bag before freezing. Water frozen lobster will last a year or better. Because the shell helps keep them fresh, wrapped lobster also keep well when frozen. Be sure to thaw lobster slowly in the refrigerator or by soaking in cool water (less than 40° F) before cooking.

There are many recipes for lobster. I prefer to cut them laterally into two halves and boil them for six or seven minutes in water, seasoned with seafood seasoning. Boiling keeps from drying the meat and helps avoid over or under cooking. However, some cooks prefer broiling or grilling. Cooked either way, a small bowl of melted margarine or butter, flavored to taste with garlic, makes an excellent dip.

Summary

Remember to follow safe diving practice when lobstering. The Florida Marine Patrol strictly enforces diver down flag laws! Navigate slowly around congregations of boats displaying diver down flags. Divers sometimes range far from their anchored boats. Consider having your divers carry individual dive flag floats. Lobstering is fun; a little extra caution will keep it that way.

Lobstering and spearfishing can sometimes be done in conjunction with each other. Divers sometimes find fish to spear while searching for lobster and sometimes catch lobster while spearfishing. When you are in lobster country prepare for both. Lobster makes an excellent addition to the spearfisherman's usual table fare of fish.

Specialty Underwater Hunting -- Scalloping

Introduction

People along the Gulf and South Atlantic Coasts believe that, "Until you've tasted fresh blue eyed (bay) scallops, you have not tasted scallops." Collecting scallops is addictive. It's the underwater equivalent to hunting Easter eggs.

Besides providing a great meal, hunting scallops improves your snorkeling skill. You become so fascinated in the hunt that you do not realize how much you are improving.

With increased land development, scallops have diminished in number and range. As late as the mid-1960's, scallops could be taken by wading with a wash tub in bays and inlets. Currently, on the Florida Gulf Coast, the only remaining area where blue eyed scallops may be legally taken begins north of the mouth of the Suwannee River (as in "way down upon the...") and extends to the Alabama State line. The only well populated beds lie in the offshore grass beds of the Big Bend and St. Joseph Bay areas of Florida.

Theories on the reason for the scallop's decline vary. Some feel that it resulted from over fishing by commercial scallop drags. Scallop dragging on grass beds is now outlawed. Other research indicates that fertilizer and pesticide laden rain water run-off caused their decline.

"Why in the world am I teaching people how to collect scallops if scallops are under such environmental stress?"

I believe that the more you know about and enjoy a resource the more you will help revive and preserve it. I subscribe to the "canary in a coal mine" view of the other creatures on this earth. If they are hurting, we may not be far behind. This does not exclude us from interacting, either by hunting, fishing, exploring, etc., with the environment and its creatures. However, it should instill in us a "caretaker" sense of responsibility.

The harm we cause comes primarily from our garbage (fertilizer and pesticide runoff, sewage, trash, manufacturing chemicals, etc.), not from our individual interaction with the environment and its creatures! If you appreciate the scallop's plight, you may cut back lawn fertilization and your use of pesticides and push for improved sewage treatment facilities.

Fertilize once every two years instead of once a year. Utilize organic gardening techniques to keep your yard looking "nice". Encourage governmental expenditures on waste treatment facilities and recycling programs. Let's bring back the scallop population and keep the canaries alive!

With scallops on the decline, how are they found? One way to find scallop beds is to rent a boat from a fish camp in scallop territory and ask for directions from the fish camp operator. With even general directions finding the scallop beds is not difficult during peak season, August. When you spot a congregation of boats with dive flags you have found the scallop beds.

Collecting Scallops

Collect scallops by snorkeling above grass beds. After you spot their "Shell Oil sign" shaped shells among the grass blades, freedive down and pick them up. Their blue eyes, which rim the open shell, often give away their location. Bare hands can be used to pick up scallops; however, gloves provide additional protection.

Scallops typically have a dark side (not the Star Wars kind, dark colored), which blends with their surroundings, and a white side, which is flatter. Their dark side usually faces up and blends with the color of the bottom. The white side usually rests on the bottom. Sometimes the best way to spot them is to catch the motion of their shell closing as you approach.

You may need to chase an occasional scallop. They sometimes swim out of your grasp. Scallops swim by rapidly opening and closing their shell, squirting water between the two halves.

Once picked up, stash your scallops in a small mesh bag. A mesh orange, onion, or potato bag serves well for collecting scallops. Larger bags, such as those used for lobster, can be used but their bulk hinders swimming. When the bag fills, return to the boat and dump your catch into an ice chest or bucket.

In Florida, a salt water fishing license is required to take scallops. Scalloping is a focused activity taking place on the grass beds were few spearfishing quarry fish species are found. Also, scallop beds are often crowded. For these reasons, scalloping and spearfishing usually do not go together. However, because it is one of the best activities for improving your freediving skill. Scalloping provides great training exercise for freedive spearfishing.

Remember to follow safe diving practice when scalloping. The Florida Marine Patrol strictly enforces diver down flag laws! Navigate slowly when you reach the scallop bed area. Snorkelers sometimes range far from their anchored boats. Consider having your snorkelers carry individual dive flag floats. Scalloping is fun; a little extra caution will keep it that way.

Preparing Scallops for the Table

After the fun of collecting them, you must clean your scallops. Cleaning scallops is not as difficult as some people contend.

First pick up a scallop by inserting a small knife blade into it's slightly open shell. The knife does not need to be sharp; a stainless or silverware type knife will do. Hold the scallop with its flatter side down and the flat hinge edge facing away from you. Cut along the upper, inside surface of the top shell, severing the muscle as close to the shell as possible. Discard the upper shell. Next, continue holding the shell with the hinge facing away from you. Use your thumb and knife to pinch the entrails in the far right corner of the shell, next to the pearl white muscle. Pull the entrails away from the muscle by pulling from far right to near left, leaving the white muscle by itself on the shell. All that remains is to slice the muscle off the lower half of the shell.

The whole process takes less than four or so seconds per scallop, once you get the hang of it. The key is to clear all of the entrails from the shell before slicing off the muscle.

A good way to prepare scallops is to sauté them in lemon, margarine, diced scallions (including the green tops), olive oil, and garlic. Great stuff!

Summary

Scalloping is a social activity. The gear is simple and collecting them is easy and fun. Anyone who can snorkel can join in the fun. Even if they are not good at snorkeling, scalloping will improve their skill faster than almost any other diving activity.

Give scalloping a try. Your taste buds will thank you.

And support clean water. Let's not loose this rare, simple pleasure!

Appendix B: Ethics, Environment, and Law

Introduction

As compared to other sections in this book, this appendix entry provides more of an editorial commentary. Its intent is to orient and educate rather than serve as a lesson. Understanding the regulatory process and pros and cons of spearfishing will help you muster and maintain support for spearfishing.

The same laws and licensing requirements that apply to other forms of recreational fishing also apply to spearfishing. However, spearfishing has antagonists. Some believe that spearfishing should be banned. Others believe that spearfishing should be allowed but restricted. Divers need to understand the various viewpoints so that they can campaign to resist unjustified restrictions on diving. By being knowledgeable on the common points upon which spearfishing is judged, spearfishermen often gain support for spearfishing. *Where fishing is allowed, spearfishing should be allowed!*

Ethics, Laws, and the Environment

Many of us like to eat fish and spearfishing provides one means of bringing fresh fish to our tables. Fish market and grocery store display cases brim with seafood taken by various means, mostly by hook and line or by net. In contrast to other means of fishing, spearfishing;

- Imposes less impact on the fishery resource;
- Is more discriminate;
- Is less environmentally damaging.

Why are there antagonists?

Some non-spearfishermen do not understand spearfishing. They believe that spearfishing allows a diver to simply choose a fish to shoot. Ignoring the telltale bubbles and the realistic limitations of the air supply, one magazine writer implied that divers on scuba can hide out for hours in camouflaged dive suits and wait to spear unsuspecting fish. This type of misinformation and lack of understanding needs correction at every opportunity. Spearfishing demands skill at "underwater hunting". Instead of shooting "the fish of his choice" a spearfisherman usually must carefully stalk his wary quarry.

How does spearfishing compare to other means of taking fish?

Recreational fishermen, skilled in both hook and line fishing as well as spearfishing, report catching more on hook and line than by spearfishing. In Florida for example, spearfishing represents an insignificant proportion of commercial fish take. Analysis of National Marine Fisheries Commission (MFC) data for Florida's commercial fish landings reveals:

- Spearfishing accounts for less than three tenths of one percent of the overall fish harvest.

- Baitfish harvest in 1990 from Tampa Bay ("Florida Sportsman", Sept. '92, p. 59) alone was 18.5 times the entire commercial spearfishing harvest for all species of fish as reported by the MFC in all of Florida!
- In the amberjack fishery, where spearfishing with powerheads is perceived as popular, the National Marine Fisheries Service reports take by spearfishing as "incidental" (Amberjack Status Report, March 1993).

Thus, spearfishing insignificantly impacts our fishing resource. If spearfishing were highly productive, more commercial fish take would be attributed to it and more commercial fishermen would use it as a means for harvesting fish.

All fishermen, hook and line as well as spear, should join together to effectively return fishing to the abundance it once enjoyed. As responsible citizens and especially as divers, we need to help revive, protect, and share our fishery resource. Fishing regulation should be based upon objective research, not emotion, sensationalism, selfishness, or misinformation. Various news releases, regulatory commission meetings, and newspaper articles, however, indicate a history of attempts to restrict diving and spearfishing.

Most recreational bag and size limits apply equally to all forms of fishing, including spearfishing. What difference does it make if a fisherman takes the bag limit for a particular fish species by spearfishing or by some other means? If the limits are managed properly from a conservational standpoint the resource should withstand fishing pressure. If not, the limits need to be reviewed and adjusted. If fish stock reduction results from too high of a recreational harvest then change the recreational limits. If excess pressure results from commercial harvest, change the commercial limits.

Spearfishing selects individual fish. There is little gamble on taking the wrong species or undersized fish. This results in insignificant waste, generically called "by-catch". By-catch is common with netting and to some extent with hook and line fishing. With a limited air supply a diver has little time to waste on illegal species, undesirable species, or on undersized fish.

In addition to virtually no by-catch, spearfishing leaves no entangling "dangerous litter" behind to entangle sea or land wildlife, such as dolphins, turtles, and birds. According to officials at the world famous Suncoast Seabird Sanctuary in Indian Rocks Beach, Florida, as of 1994, not one bird injury treated by them had been attributed to spearfishing. The majority of injuries result from nets, hooks, and monofilament line.

In most states hunting on land remains legal while trapping, with its indiscriminate nature, has been outlawed or severely restricted. Spearfishing (underwater hunting), when compared to other means of fishing, is significantly more discriminate and the least environmentally disruptive method for taking fish.

Divers help keep the environment clean. Sport divers often remove and properly dispose of abandoned fishing line, plastic bags, fishing lead, and other "dangerous litter". Dive clubs in some areas participate in organized environmental cleanup events. Others carry on year round cleanup competitions. Not just a "flash in the pan" high publicity event, with some clubs this cleaning process goes on year round. Divers accumulate points throughout the year for picking up litter on dives and record their "take" on competition forms. Annual awards, based upon accumulated points, are presented. Divers get no publicity or recognition outside of the club. They simply do it. One such club, the Sunshine Fins, is made up of mostly spearfishermen who appreciate the importance of improving our environment. It and many clubs like it accept the responsibility of cleaning our oceans.

Some fishermen carry negative attitudes toward spearfishing. At one National Marine Fisheries scoping meeting a fisherman stated that he was against spearfishing because once "a boat full of spearfishermen" dropped off on his fishing spot; shot several amberjack; and then left him to his now disturbed fishing spot. His animosity is understandable! But, he also acknowledged becoming upset anytime other hook and line fishermen anchor next to him, horning in on his fishing spot.

What we need for these kinds of situations is not anti-spearfishing regulation but rather an Anti-Jerk Law! (Send me any ideas you have on the wording for such a law.) In the mean time, show common courtesy by avoiding fishing, either by spear or by hook and line, on a spot already occupied.

Discussion arises at times about spearfishing while using scuba. Some feel that spearfishing on scuba gives an unfair advantage to the diver. Perhaps some divers can freedive and spearfish to depths of 30 feet or more; however, most divers cannot. Should they be restricted from enjoying fresh fish because they are not super athletes? Divers on scuba do not have hours of bottom time except in very shallow water! They have the additional impediment of the telltale bubbles from their exhaled air and they are slowed by the drag of the gear. It's a wonder that they can get within shooting range of a fish at all.

Freediving works best in clear, relatively shallow water. Some dive areas simply do not provide shallow enough depths or sufficient water clarity to allow effective freediving. Additionally, some divers, concerned about shallow water blackout, prefer not to freedive. Scuba provides the technology for divers of various physical abilities to enjoy spearfishing in a wide range of diving conditions. It should be recognized and accepted, at least by the fish eating public, as an environmentally friendly means of taking fish for our tables.

Summary

Are there abuses in spearfishing? Surely isolated instances occur. Just as we see dead fish thrown by fishermen on bridge sidewalks to die in the sun, spearfishermen can break laws too. However, current spearfishing methods are no more prone to abuse than other means of fishing. Let's curb isolated abuses through peer pressure, education, and the enforcement of general fishing regulations, not needless restriction targeted at spearfishing or certain spearfishing gear.

Influence and lead by example. Know the pros and cons of spearfishing. Show respect for the environment by taking only what you need. Be discrete. Respect other divers and fishermen by not spearfishing near them. Make as big of a show of the plastic bags you remove from the environment as you do of that ten pound *fishious deliciousoso* you spear. Take an active interest in improving our environment!

AND PROMOTE: *Where fishing is allowed, spearfishing should be allowed!*

Appendix C: Manufacturer Reference

AB Biller Company: Speargun and spearfishing accessory manufacturer, including spearshafts, speartips, stringers, powerheads, bands and band material, pole spears, and Hawaiian slings. Distributor the *Sea Hornet* line of mahogany, teak, and stainless barrel spearguns.

AB Biller
PO Box 316

Bloomingdale, IL 60108
(800)443-1123

ACL Enterprises: Manufacturer and distributor of *Auto Coil*, coiled monofilament spearshaft and accessory line.

ACL Enterprises
PO Box 37945

Jacksonville, FL 32205
(904)387-4746

Aquatic Specialties: Manufacturer and distributor of the *"Equalizer"* automatic lobster snare.

Aquatic Specialties
2160B Mariner Blvd.

Springhill, FL 34609
(904)686-4193

A-Plus Marine Supply, Inc.: Distributor of spearguns, spearshafts, speartips, and other diving and spearfishing accessories. Distributes a broad line of guns including Cressi, Mares, and other pneumatics and JBL, AB Biller, and other band powered guns.

TJS
2234 16th Avenue N

St. Petersburg, FL 33713
(813)323-1251

B&B Products: Manufacturer of spearshafts, speartips, powerheads, and heavy duty safety pin style stringers.

B&B Products
PO Box 21207

St. Petersburg, FL 33742
(813)546-2888

Beuchat, USA: General dive gear and spearfishing equipment distributor. Distributes a popular line of pneumatic spearguns.

Beuchat, USA
1321 NW 65th Place

Ft. Lauderdale, FL 33309
(305)978-1204

Blue Water Hunter: Retailer specializing spearfishing equipment, including custom spearguns and low buoyancy wetsuits.

> Blue Water Hunter   Goleta, CA 93117
> 5608 Hollister Ave. Suite B (800)452-6696

Diving Equipment Corp.: Manufacturer of telescoping pole spears and bang sticks.

> Diving Equipment Corp.   Cleveland, OH 44103
> 4811 Carnegie Ave.   (800)847-0714

JBL Enterprises, Inc.: Manufacturer of spearguns and a full line of spearfishing accessories, including spearshafts, speartips, stringers, powerheads, pole spears, and Hawaiian slings. Manufacturer of the popular JBL aluminum spearguns.

> JBL Enterprises, Inc.   Orange, CA 92666
> 426 W. Almond Ave.   (714)633-0860

Mares USA: Manufacture of a full line of diving equipment, including spearguns and accessories. Known for their pneumatic spearguns.

> Mares USA   Boulder, CO 80301
> 4801 North 3rd Street   (800)874-3236 ext. 600
>   (303)530-2000

Marine Diving Distributors: Manufacturer and distributor of a full line of dive gear, spearfishing equipment, and accessories., including pole spears, Hawaiian slings, stringers, speartips, powerheads, and *Deep See* wooden spearguns.

> Marine Diving Distributors   Tampa, FL 33634
> 6001 Johns Road, Suite 701   (813)932-9478

Most Atlantic Company: Distributor of the Russian *Sea Bear* pneumatic spearguns and laser sights.

> Most Atlantic Company   Cuyahoga Falls, OH 44223
> 3656 State Road   (800)860-1211

Ray Odor Diving Service: Manufacturer of spearshafts, pole spears, speartips, powerheads, stringers, and other spearfishing accessories.

> Ray Odor Diving Service   Tampa, FL 33696
> PO Box 350386   (813)971-3368

Riffe International: Manufacturer and distributor of spearguns, float buoy rigs, and other spearfishing equipment. Known for the Riffe teak barrel blue water spearguns and freediving equipment.

Riffe International   San Clemente, CA 92673
1030 Calle Sombra   (800)773-2748

Sea Search, Inc.: Manufacture and distributor of the slim-lined Sea Stinger detachable spearshaft and pole spear tips.

Sea Search, Inc.   Jacksonville, FL 32216
1736 St. Johns Bluff Rd.   (904)642-0662

Spearfishing Specialties: Distributor of spearfishing equipment including spearshafts, spare spearshaft holders, and custom spearfishing accessories. Specializes in custom teak spearguns.

Spearfishing Specialties   St. Petersburg, FL 33710
5335 3rd Ave. North   (813)323-7686

Sport Divers Manufacturing: Manufacturer and distributor of a full line of dive gear, spearfishing equipment, and accessories. Products include pole spears, stringers, speartips, sleds, and spearguns.

Sport Divers Manufacturing Miami, FL 33181
1923 NE 150 Street   (800)327-0244

TJS: Manufacturer of spearfishing equipment including slim-line detachable speartips, spare spearshaft holders, line reels, and other custom spearfishing accessories.

TJS   St. Petersburg, FL 33713
2234 16th Avenue N   (813)323-1251

Trident Diving Equipment: Distributor of spearguns, spearshafts, speartips, and other spearfishing accessories.

Trident Diving Equipment   Chatsworth, CA 91311
9616 Owensmouth Ave.   (800)776-6449

Appendix D: Answers to review questions

Chapter 1:
1. Why is it necessary for a diver to be self reliant before taking up spearfishing? (Because he is responsible for his own safety, and because of the presence of spearfishing equipment, the safety of other divers.)
2. List five basic skills required for spearfishing on scuba. (Mask removal, buoyancy control, monitoring air, depth, dive table proficiency, continuous breathing)
3. List two advanced skills recommended for spearfishing. (Navigation, CPR & first aid training)
4. T/F A diver must be a conditioned athlete before taking up spearfishing? (F)
5. What is freediving or apnea diving? (Diving while breath holding.)
6. What is shallow water blackout? (Loss of consciousness while freediving.)
7. How can risk from shallow water blackout be reduced? (Dive in alternating buddy pairs; avoid hyperventilating with more than three breaths prior to a dive; and, dive in water less than 50 feet.)

Chapter 2:
1. What is the overall consideration in the basic gear you chose to use while spearfishing? (Choose gear you like and with which you are comfortable.)
2. Name three features to look for in choosing a mask for use in spearfishing. (Comfortable fit, good seal, and does not fog.)
3. Why does a black skirt or color that prevents light from entering from the sides help underwater vision? (Reduces glare.)
4. Large, stiff bladed fins are best for divers with strong legs? (T)
5. How are strap fins modified to prevent the straps from slipping or becoming entangled? (Tape the strap ends.)
6. What is the objective in selecting a snorkel without a purge valve or "dry" feature? (Reduced drag.)
7. How does a snorkel contribute to "dead air space"? (By increasing the volume of un-exhaled air.)
8. Why might it be advantageous to wear your snorkel on your right side instead of the accepted left side? (Puts the snorkel and second stage hose on the same side of the head, reducing interference with head motion and the possibility of entanglement.)
9. Why should the snorkel be worn on the mask, and not carried in a bcd pocket or on a clip? (Upon surfacing it may be difficult to reach and use with hands full of spearfishing equipment and fish.)
10. List six considerations in choosing a bcd for use in spearfishing. (Bladder-less construction to reduce bulkiness and minimize trapped air; Shoulder releases to simplify removal; Large pockets with positive closures to store extra equipment; "D" rings for attaching extra gear; Good inflation and deflation system with easy low pressure hose disconnect; Good fit but large enough to allow for wearing with an exposure suit).
11. List five features to look for in a regulator used for spearfishing. (Must breathe easily and dryly in all attitudes and under various conditions, i.e. when you are horizontal, upside down, on your back, on either side, upright, and swimming hard; Reputable, available service (Some older, used regulators or uncommon brands are not easily serviced); At least 3 low and 1 high pressure ports on the first stage; Good first stage manifold design with hoses arranged sensibly; The fewer the number of swivels and "O" rings the better.)
12. What is the most popular size of scuba cylinder and from what material are they made? (Aluminum 80)
13. List the three types of primary weighting systems: (bcd integrated, pouch belt, and strap belt.)

14. List five pieces of miscellaneous gear useful in spearfishing. (Gloves for hand protection. Garden gloves will work but dive gloves dry better and allow better dexterity; A small dive light attached by a lanyard and tucked away in a bcd pocket for use in looking under dark ledges; A knife in a position where it can be removed with either hand. (Some spearfishermen attach it with electrical tie wraps or with Velcro ® straps to the bcd's manual inflator hose. Be careful not to interfere with the inflator hose's action. A small marker buoy and weight, coiled up and tucked away in a bcd pocket, for use in marking a spot to return to; A tucked away mesh bag comes in handy when collecting trash or when an unexpected lobster turns up.)

Chapter 3:

1. For each of the speargun components listed below, fill in the matching number from the diagram.
   Speartip: _____
   Line Slide: _____
   Muzzle: _____
   Spearshaft: _____
   Safety: _____
   Shaft lock mechanism housing: _____
   Cocking stock: _____
   Cocking plate or cocking butt: _____
   Handle housing: _____
   Knuckle guard: _____
   Line release: _____
   Trigger: _____
   Line: _____
   Barrel: _____
   Power bands: _____
   Line keeper: _____
2. T/F A longer gun and spearshaft generally provides longer range and accuracy than a shorter gun. (T)
3. T/F A longer gun is easier to sweep through the water and is more maneuverable than a shorter gun. (F)
4. T/F When a spear is loaded in a pneumatic gun, the gun is also cocked and ready to shoot. (T)
5. T/F Guns are sometimes distinguished variously as wood or metal guns and as pneumatic or band powered guns. (T)
6. T/F Freeshaft guns and line guns are the basic gun configurations. (T)
7. Which gun type, freeshaft or line gun, typically has the most range, spearshaft speed, and accuracy. (Freeshaft gun)
8. Give the two most common types of spearshaft propulsion method. (Band and pneumatic)
9. List the five types of line material used on line guns. (Braided nylon, Kevlar, or Dacron line, stainless steel cable, shock cord, monofilament line, and "slinky" cord represent typical line materials.)
10. Give three ways to help avoid becoming "caught in the bight". (Face the fish as you fight it; Avoid spearfishing around obstacles; Use a line no longer than the effective range of the gun; Keep hands, feet, etc. clear of loops in the line.)
11. List the five situations where being towed on a line gun by a fish can be dangerous. (Deeper than is safe; Into an overhead environment; For a longer period of time than planned for the dive; Around an obstruction, posing a danger of becoming "wrapped up"; Up faster than a safe ascent rate.)
12. Name two types of line extending line gun options. (Reel gun, float buoy rig, butt wrap)
13. What distinguishes a double-barreled gun from a combination gun, both of which carry two spearshafts? (The double-barreled gun has two trigger mechanisms and can carry two cocked spearshafts.)

14. T/F With line detached from the spearshaft a hybrid line gun's range, spearshaft speed, and accuracy approach that of a freeshaft gun. (T)

Chapter 4:

1. What distinguishes a speargun from a pole spear or Hawaiian sling? (Spearguns have a mechanical catch for holding the spearshaft in a cocked position; pole spears and Hawaiian slings are manually held in a "cocked" position.)
2. List three types of speartips used on pole spears. (Paralyzer, hinged barb, trident, detachable, powerhead.)
3. What type of configuration works well for taking large fish with a pole spear? (Break-away)
4. T/F Maximum range on a pole spear is about two thirds the length of the spear. (T)
5. T/F Hawaiian slings have been called the underwater equivalent to combining a sling shot with a bow and arrow. (T)
6. What type of tip is typically used on a Hawaiian sling spear? (Hinged barb.)
7. Briefly describe one technique of using a Hawaiian sling. (Pull and release or pull back and hold.)
8. What are the advantages of pole spears and Hawaiian slings over mechanical release type spearguns? (They are less prone to mechanical failure and are more quickly readied for a shooting.)
9. What are the disadvantages of pole spears and Hawaiian slings? (They do not have the range and require more skill to use.)

Chapter 5:

1. Name the three types of metal typically used in spearshafts and accessories. (Spring stainless steel, stainless steel, and non-stainless steel.)
2. T/F Longer spearshafts are used for longer range. Heavier spearshafts are used for larger fish. (T)
3. List five types of spear accessories. (Spare spearshaft holders, line slides, line slide backing plates, hinged barb hold-down retainers, spearshaft pins, speartips and powerheads, thread and catch adapters.)
4. Why is it important to keep accessories firmly tightened? (Avoid damage to the threads and avoid loss of equipment and fish.)
5. Why should spearshafts for guns made by one manufacturer not be used on guns made by another manufacturer? (They may not hold in the shaft catch, resulting in accidental firing of the gun.)
6. List two spearshaft related problems which can cause missed shots. (Bent spearshaft, bent barb.)
7. Match speartip components to the following diagram:
   Point _____
   Barbs _____
   Barb spreader _____
   Barb retainer _____
   Tip shaft _____
   Threaded collar _____
8. How should a speartip or other accessory be tightened on a spearshaft? (Using two pair of pliers with the spearshaft removed from the gun.)
9. Generally when are detachable tips used? (On large fish or fish with soft flesh.)
10. List four types of speartips. (Hinged barb tips with a single point, detachable, paralyzer, flat fork, trident.)
11. In spearfishing, on what type of fish are powerheads generally used. (Large powerful fish such as amberjack.)
12. When used on a line gun, what is the effect on the gun's range when using a powerhead. (It significantly reduces it.)
13. How can a cave diving reel be used during a safety stop? (To send up a surface float to help the boat operator locate the divers.)

14. What is a toss buoy? (A buoy with a weight and length of line which is used to mark a dive site.)
15. List three devices for carrying game. (Safety pin stringer, line stringer, game bag, pole spear.)
16. Is a fish removed from the spearshaft before or after the fish is on the stringer? (After.)
17. Why should tow sleds not be used by divers on scuba? (Danger of rapid ascent and of being lost.)

Chapter 6:
1. Why is a check list important when preparing for a dive trip? (Helps keep you from forgetting gear and preparation details.)
2. Why is it important to file a float plan? (So that someone on land knows when you are expected to return, a description of the boat, and the general vicinity of where you plan to dive in case you are overdue.)
3. What is the purpose for marking measurements on your speargun? (To help assess fish size underwater and avoid shooting undersized fish.)
4. What do the terms "kill shot" and "stone shot" mean? (To kill a fish with one shot so that it does not fight and tear off the spearshaft.)
5. When stringing a fish, how is a floating gun kept under control? (The diver slides his arm through the bands.)
6. How is a small fighting fish subdued? (By pinning it to the bottom and stringing it through its eyes or gills.)
7. How are medium and large fish subdued? (By disabling it with a poke from a knife in a vital area before stringing.)
8. Before reaching under a ledge to retrieve a "holed up" fish, what precaution should be taken. (Look the situation over to verify that there is no dangerous marine life under the ledge with the fish.)
9. What effect does a fish's swim bladder have on a diver's buoyancy as the diver surfaces with a stringer of fish? (It increases buoyancy.)
10. What can be done with a stringer of fish that is causing you to ascend too fast? (Release the entire stringer, allowing it to surface ahead of you.)
11. What is "ranging"? (Diving by covering an area with the boat un-anchored but following the diver.)
12. T/F Buddy pairs can either swim shoulder to shoulder or swim with one leading and the other following. (T)

Chapter 7:
1. In general, how is a speargun handled? (Like a loaded firearm.)
2. List the safety considerations in terms of speargun maintenance. (Make sure spearguns are maintained on a regular basis; Before each use verify that they function properly.)
3. List the precautions when handling a speargun. (Always load guns in the water, pointed in a safe direction; Never discharge a speargun out of the water; Keep the safety on until ready to shoot; Before you shoot, make sure that you know what you are shooting at and what is behind it; Avoid spearfishing in murky water; Never spearfish in crowded areas; When passing a gun to someone, always hand it unloaded and butt first, with the speartip facing away from you.)
4. List the precautions when transporting and storing spearguns. (Transport spearguns and spare spearshafts with protective covers over the tips and position them so that they will not damage other equipment or cause injury if the tip cover comes off; Store spearguns in a location secured from children.)
5. Describe five indicators of a properly functioning speargun. (1) The spearshaft locks positively in the catch and trigger mechanism; 2) With line guns the line is firmly attached to the spearshaft and the gun, and the mechanical line keeper holds the line securely; 3) The shaft catch notch on the spearshaft is free from wear; 4) On band guns the band material and "wishbone" are in good shape; 5) Barrel, muzzle, and handle components are free from cracks, corrosion, rot, and free play; 6) The safety works smoothly and

positively; 7) Speartips are sharp, secure, and the barbs function as designed; and, 8) When firing, the trigger mechanism pulls smoothly.)

6. T/F Murky water is safer for spearfishing than clear water. (F)
7. T/F Spearfishermen, as a matter of etiquette, should leave the scenic dive sites to sightseeing type divers. (T)
8. When should a gun be cocked? (After the diver is in the water.)
9. Why should spearguns not be fired out of water? (They were not designed to be fired out of water so it is hard on them mechanically. With line guns the spearshaft can recoil back toward the person who shoots the gun. The spearshaft can carry dangerously in air.)
10. When should a gun's safety be switched to the "fire" position? (When ready to shoot.)
11. What is a spearshaft caddie? (A seal-able tube in which spearshafts are carried.)
12. What maintenance and storage procedures should be followed for spearguns? (Wash it with fresh water; allow to dry; inspect for wear and have serviced if necessary; lubricate the shaft catch mechanism with silicone or other spray lubricant; store in a secure, dark, dry, well-ventilated location.)
13. What is the number one cause of deterioration in synthetic materials? (Sunlight with exposure to petroleum based lubricants and solvents a close enough second to accept as an answer.)
14. List five precautions to reduce chance encounters with or injury from dangerous marine life when spearfishing?
    - Always swim calmly and observe your surroundings. Be alert for dangerous marine life or conditions (clear water and calm seas help when looking for dangerous marine life);
    - Promptly remove speared fish from the water;
    - Do not carry speared fish with you;
    - Do not shoot fish when sharks or barracuda are present;
    - Calmly get out of the water if you feel threatened by a shark or other marine life; (Remember, sharks and barracuda can out swim even the fastest swimmer so retreat calmly and remain facing them.)
    - Avoid touching the bottom where urchins, fire coral, and abrasive rock is found;
    - Never reach into a crevice or under a ledge;
    - If a barracuda, shark, or jewfish takes a fish you have speared, let them keep it. Neither fish nor spearshaft is worth getting injured over;
    - Do not dive in areas being fished by fishermen using chum;
    - Learn to use and carry a powerhead for protection;
    - Do not shoot barracuda, shark, or other potentially dangerous marine life;
    - Do not dive in areas known for dangerous marine life;
    - Do not feed or harass dangerous marine life;
    - If you feel uncomfortable during a dive, trust your sixth sense and calmly get out of the water.
15. How can you help remove a non-spearfisherman's fear about spearguns? (Show them a little bit about your speargun and explain spearfishing to them.)

Chapter 8:
1. What sources can be used to locate dive sites? (Books, charts, and fishing location lists, available from book stores, dive centers, fishing tackle supply stores, and other spearfishermen.)
2. How can you find your own "secret" spots? (By using commercially available dive site list as a seed list and searching near "known" dive sites.)
3. What is the main rule when diving from someone else's boat? (Be considerate.)
4. What services do dive clubs provide? (They are a source of information on diving, they organize diving and non-diving events, help shape dive regulation, and provide various community services.)

5.   What benefit is there in attending or participating in spearfishing tournaments?   (Exposure to experts, tournaments hone a spearfisherman's skill.)

Appendix E: About the author

Allen Patrick, a Florida native, has spearfished actively since 1963. He directed the Southern Open Derby Spearfishing and Photography contest in 1993 and 1994 and the St. Pete Open Spearfishing Tournament in 1995. Very active in organized diving he has held several offices including: 1) President of the Florida Skin Divers Association; 2) President of the St. Petersburg Underwater Club; 3) Tampa Bay area coordinator of the Florida Coalition of Concerned Sport Divers; 4) Member of the Spiny Lobster Advisory Panel to the Gulf of Mexico Fishery Management Council; and, 5) Member of the Sunshine Fins Dive Club. In 1993, the West Coast Council of Dive Clubs presented Allen with the Norm Wymann/Poppa Taylor Sportsmanship award for his contributions to diving. He actively and effectively campaigns to protect diving rights, particularly  spearfishing rights. A certified diver since 1968, his current qualifications include: PADI Scuba Instructor, PADI Medic First Aid Instructor, USCG licensed Captain, USCG certified Safety Drill Master, certified regulator repair and cylinder inspection technician, Colgate Offshore Sailing School Sailing Instructor, and hyperbaric chamber attendant. Past professional experience includes serving as manager of development, support, training, and documentation for a major information services corporation. He currently works as a business automation consultant, independent scuba and sailing instructor, boat captain, computer consultant, and writer.

Glossary

Note: **Italicized** *words found in descriptions of terms in this glossary also appear as individual glossary definitions.*

Band catch notch or band notch: Notch milled into a *spearshaft* that catches the *power band's wishbone* when a speargun is cocked. Some band catch notches are welded onto the shaft to avoid weakening the shaft.

Bang stick: A rod or handle onto which a powerhead is attached. These are usually carried for protection from predators.

Barb: A hinged or milled notch protruding from a spearshaft that points in the opposite direction to the spearshaft's point. The barb prevents a speared fish from sliding off the end of the spearshaft. See also *flipper* and *flopper*.

Braille dive: Dive with poor visibility, not a recommended condition for spearfishing.

Barrel: The part of a speargun that holds the muzzle and handle together rigidly, serves as a spearshaft guide, and contributes to the gun's flotation characteristics and its length.

Breakaway rig: A lineshaft attached to a long line leading to a buoy on the surface. When a fish is speared it tows the line and buoy. When the fish tires the diver hauls it up from his position at the surface. This rig is popular with freedivers, especially when spearing large fish. Attaching a buoyed line to a detachable tip on a pole spear provides a variation on this rig.

Break: A sharp change in bottom contour displayed on an electronic depth recorder. A break usually indicates a submerged ledge or wreck. See also *fish show*.

Cock: On band powered guns: after loading a spearshaft it refers to pulling the bands back into the *band catch notches*. On pneumatic and spring powered guns the one motion of loading also cocks these guns. See also *load*.

Cocking butt: An extended *gun butt* , composed of the cocking stock and cocking plate, that aids in cocking a speargun.

Cocking plate: A widened cap which fits onto the cocking stock. It provides a more comfortable surface when placing the gun against the thigh, hip, or chest to cock the gun.

Cocking stock: The part of a speargun that extends behind the handle and to which the *cocking plate* is attached. Sometimes this is called an extension.

Detachable tip: A speartip that detaches from the spearshaft after penetrating a fish but remains connected to the gun or a buoy by a cable.

Discharging: Shooting a speargun is the same as *firing*.

Firing: Shooting a speargun is the same as *discharging*.

Fish show: A display on a boat's electronic depth recorder indicating a congregation of fish. See also *break*.

Flipper: A hinged *barb* attached either to a spearshaft or to a speartip.

Flopper: Same as *flipper*.

Freeshaft: A speargun spearshaft that is not attached by line or cable to the gun or a surface buoy.

Full pull: A full stringer or game bag full of fish.

Bottom management or site management: Strategically spearfishing a dive site in such a way that the most fish can be taken.

Gun butt: The end of a speargun behind the handle. It includes the stock extension and *cocking butt*. A gun butt usually has a pad or plate to distribute pressure when cocking the speargun. See also *cocking butt*.

Handle housing: The part of a speargun that holds the shaft catch mechanism, and includes a handle, trigger, line release, and safety.

Holed up: Used to refer to a speared fish that has run under a ledge or into a wreck and wedged itself in such a way that it is difficult to remove.

Keeper: A fish or lobster legally large enough to keep. Some fish have no minimum size limit. The limit for those that do varies by species.

Kill shot; to hit a fish in a vital area that either kills or incapacitates it. Same as *roll* and *stone*.

Kill spot, spot on a fish that, if hit with a spear, results in a kill shot.

Leading: When *tracking* a moving fish, the technique of aiming just ahead of where the spear should strike.

Line clip: A friction clip attached to the underside of a speargun's barrel which holds the line for storage while a line gun is loaded. When the gun discharges the line pulls out of the clip. See *line release and line keeper*.

Line keeper: A protrusion on the *muzzle* that holds *shooting slack* when wrapped between the *line release* or *line clip* and the front of the gun.

Line release: A mechanical finger that holds the line for storage when a line gun is loaded and which releases the line when the trigger is pulled. A line release differs from a *line clip* in that it operates mechanically when the gun fires rather than from spring tension. See *line keeper and line clip*.

Line slide: A metal ring or loop that fits on a spearshaft to which a line attaches to keep the spearshaft attached to the gun. A *slide stop* prevents the line slide from sliding off the end of the spearshaft.

Lineshaft: A spearshaft to which a line or cable is attached. Usually the line attaches to a *line slide*. On some it is attached to a hole drilled into the back end of the spearshaft.

Load: To place a spearshaft in the gun. With band powered guns the spearshaft fits into the muzzle and snaps into the shaft catch mechanism. The bands must be cocked before the gun can be discharged. On pneumatic and spring powered guns the one motion of loading also cocks these guns. See also *cock*.

Mexican rig: Same as *breakaway rig*.

Muzzle: The muzzle is the firing end of the barrel. It is typically made of plastic or aluminum, the muzzle holds the bands and provides a guide for the spearshaft. On some wood guns the muzzle is integral to the *barrel*.

Numbers: Dive site location referenced by loran coordinates or by latitude and longitude.

Powerhead: A cylindrical steel chamber with a firing pin that attaches to a spearshaft. When loaded with the proper caliber ammunition cartridge it discharges when the spear strikes a fish. This provides a very effective knock-out concussion for killing large fish. A powerhead consists of: 1) A cylindrical steel cartridge chamber, 2) A firing pin, 3) A safety, and, 4) A coupling for attaching the powerhead to a spearshaft, bangstick, or speargun powerhead holder.

Power band: Elastic surgical tubing fitted with a *wishbone* that powers a spearshaft.

Ride: 1) To arrange an invitation to go spearfishing on someone's boat; 2) To be dragged around by a large line gun speared fish, as in, "That fish took me for a ride!"

Power band: 1) Surgical tubing sling; 2) Wishbone retainer rings; 3) Wishbone.

Roll, roll over: To kill a fish instantly with one shot.

Rubber: Same as *power band*.

Shooting line: This term refers to the relatively small diameter line or cable that attaches between the spearshaft and speargun. Comparable to a fishing leader, shooting line also designates a small line used for shooting slack when attached to a heavier line such as a *breakaway* or *tow rig* line. Wrapped between the *spearshaft, muzzle,* and *line release* it provides minimal resistance by releasing as the spearshaft shoots from the gun.

Shooting slack: Refers to the length of *shooting line*, usually referred to in number of *wraps of shooting slack*. One loop, from front of gun to *line release* and back to the front, counts as one wrap.

Shaft catch notch: The notch milled into the end of a spearshaft that locks into a speargun's mechanical release.

Shaft stock: The metal round stock from which spearshafts are cut and milled.

Slide stop: A small raised area, milled into a spearshaft, which prevents the *line slide* from sliding off the end of a spearshaft when a line gun discharges.

Slide: See *line slide*.

Slip tip: See *detachable tip*.

Smoke: When a fish stirs up silt and sediment, making visibility poor.

Speargun: Mechanical spearguns utilize a mechanical shaft catch and release trigger mechanism. Pictured below is a generic band powered speargun.

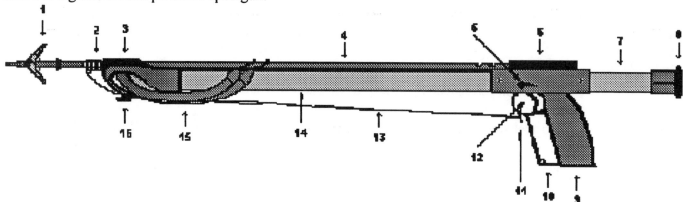

1. Speartip	9. Handle housing
2. Line slide	10. Knuckle guard
3. Muzzle	11. Line release
4. Spearshaft	12. Trigger
5. Safety	13. Line
6. Shaft catch housing	14. Barrel
7. Cocking stock or extension	15. Power bands
8. Cocking plate or cocking butt	16. Line keeper or holder

Spearshaft: A typical spearshaft consists of a *speartip*, with its *barbs*, the *shaft stock*, which comprises the length of the spearshaft, *band notches, slide stop*, and a *shaft catch notch*.

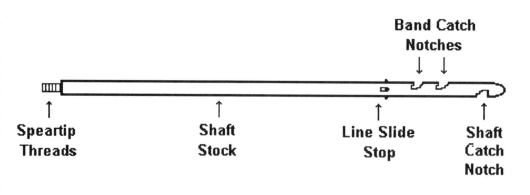

Spearpoint: The sharp point on the end of a *speartip*. Some manufacturers use the terms *spearpoint* and *speartip* interchangeably.

Speartip: A generic speartip consists of round metal stock into which a sharp *spearpoint* is milled and one or more *barbs* attached. They can either be threaded onto a spearshaft or built directly into the spearshaft. Speartips come in a variety of designs including rock point, paralyzer, trident, detachable, etceteras. Some manufacturers use the terms *spearpoint* and *speartip* interchangeably.

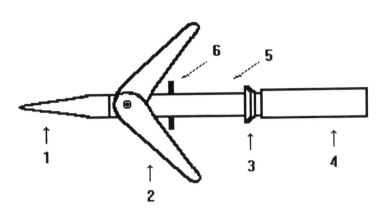

1. Spearpoint	4. Threaded collar
2. Barb or flipper	5. Speartip shaft
3. Barb retainer	6. Barb spreader

Stone: See *kill shot*.

Tickle stick: A 3/16" to 5/16" by 2' to 3' plastic or aluminum rod used to coach lobster from their hiding place. Tickle sticks are usually straight; however, some have a slight bend about 4" from one end.

Tow rig: A spearshaft attached by wire cable or nylon shooting line to a length of rope with an eye splice grip. A section of garden hose provides padding for the eye splice grip. After shooting a fish the diver holds onto the eye splice grip and is towed by the fish. Should hanging on too dangerous, the rope is released. The spearshaft and line are lost, but not the entire gun. This rig is primarily used in the North Central Gulf of Mexico for shooting amberjack in deep water.

Tracking: When aiming at a moving fish, the act of following a fish through the water by sweeping the speargun through the water to keep it on target.

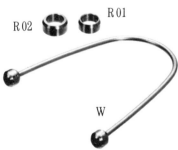

Umbilical: The tether of air hose attaching a surface supplied air diver to the surface compressor.

Wishbone: Wire, nylon, or monofilament part of a speargun *power band* which fits into the spearshaft's *band notch*.

Wishbone and retainer rings.
Courtesy of AB Biller Company.

Wrap of shooting line: Measure of the length of *shooting line*. One loop, from front of gun to *line release* and back to the front, being counted as one wrap.

Bibliography

1. **Allyn, Rube:** *Dictionary of Fishes,* Eleventh Edition, Great Outdoors Publishing, Co., St. Petersburg, FL, 1981. This excellent and inexpensive fish identification book includes drawings, descriptions, catch record, habitat, and food value information.

2. **Andren, Carl**: *The LORAN/GPS Program*, Andren Software Co., P.O. Box 33117, Indialantic, FL 32903. Available in DOS or Windows version, this is a software program for storing, organizing, and plotting dive site coordinates in either LORAN numbers or Latitude and Longitude.

3. *Audubon Society Field guide to North American Fishes, Whales, and Dolphins*, Alfred A. Knof, Inc., New York, NY, 1983. Pocket sized (if you have large pockets) fish reference with 684 photographs and descriptions.

4. **Balder, A. P.:** *Complete Manual of Skin Diving*, Macmillan Company, NY, 1971. LCC Card Number 68-23060. This is one of the earlier "how to" books on diving. It includes chapters on all aspects of diving. Spearfishing, along with various other special interests, is covered in Chapter Seven of this book as a "special diving activity".

5. **Blue Water Video, Inc.:** *The Art of Spearfishing*, 1991 (Contact AB Biller Company, (708)529-2776). This thirty minute color video includes footage of actual spearfishing and makes a good case for spearfishing as an environmentally healthy means of harvesting fish.

6. **Bolduc, John**: "Missing Keys for Crawfish," *Florida Sportsman*, Wickstrom Publishers, Inc., Miami, FL, July, 1994. This article describes catching spiny lobster in other than the Florida Keys. It includes information on where to go on Florida's East coast, laws, and use of tickle sticks and nets.

7. **Christensen, Lot:** "Struggling with the ethics of Spearfishing," *SCUBA Times,* August, 1994. Article pointing out the limited bycatch of spearfishing as compared to the high bycatch of shrimping and other means of fishing. It also discusses responsible spearfishing.

8. **Cropp, Ben:** *Shark Hunters,* Macmillan Company, 1971. Australian photographer and film maker Ben Cropp relates adventures he encountered as he filmed for various National Geographic, BBC, Australian, and ABC documentaries. Originally published in 1964, then updated and republished in 1969 before being published in the United States in 1971, the book focuses on spearfishing for sharks. However, it also weaves tips on: 1) Spearfishing; 2) Wreck hunting; 3) Shark, moray, and fish feeding; and, 4) Dealing with sea snakes. Written in days when sportsmanship was interpreted differently, the book provides experience through reading, especially for techniques used on big fish and in dealing with dangerous marine life.

9. **DeLoach, Ned:** *Diving Guide to Underwater Florida, 8th Edition,* New World Publications, Jacksonville, FL, 1993. A recommended book on Florida diving. Includes dive site locations and descriptions of both salt and fresh water diving.

10. *Encyclopedia of Recreational Diving,* International PADI, Inc., 1993. This encyclopedia covers physics, physiology, equipment, environment, and special diving activities. This is a highly recommended reference.

11. **Escudo Productions**: *Successful Spearfishing*; Escudo Productions, Route 2, Box 560-A, Tallahassee, FL 32311; (800)776-1584; 1991. Excellent introductory spearfishing video. (Run time: 30 min.)

12. **Eyles, Carlos**: *The Last of the Blue Water Hunters,* Watersport Publishing, Inc. San Diego, CA, 1991. Book covering impressive spearfishing feats of some of the pioneers of diving in California and Florida. It includes anecdotes about diving adventures. It weaves in tips on spearfishing technique.

13. **Gilliam, Bret:** "Freediving Hazards, You Want to Play, You've Got to Pay," *SCUBA Times,* August, 1994. Article exploring the dangers of freediving. This issue of SCUBA Times includes several other articles on freediving.

14. **Greenberg, Idaz and Jerry:** *Waterproof Guide to Corals and Fishes,* Seahawk Press, Miami, FL, 1977. This handy fish identification guide booklet to will fit in your dive bag and it is waterproof.

15. **Haas, Hans:** *Challenging the Deep,* George G. Harrap & Co. Ltd., 1972. This book chronicles of one of the pioneers of diving, covers early history of diving, and includes spearfishing anecdotes and other diving adventures.

16. **Hoover, Pierce:** "Aluminum or Steel?", *Sport Diver Magazine,* Winter Park, FL, December, 1994. This article describes the features of and presents pros and cons for various sizes of aluminum and steel tanks.

17. **Humann, Paul:** *Reef Fish Identification,* New World Publications, Jacksonville, FL, 1993, (904)737-6558. Fish identification book with color photographs and descriptions of over 300 common and some not so common reef fish.

18. *International Sailing Supply Fish and Dive Charts,* International Sailing Supply, Punta Gorda, FL, 1991, (813)7626. These charts are re-makes of NOAA navigational charts with fishing and diving locations provided.

19. **Ivanovic, Ivan S.:** *Modern Spearfishing,* Henry Regnery Company, Chicago, IL; 1975. First published in 1954, this book addresses the sport of spearfishing. It touches on all aspects of early spearfishing technology and technique.

20. **Jarman, Colin:** *The Essential Knot Book,* International Marine, P.O. Box 220, Camden, Maine 04843, 1986. Clear and succinct book covering how to tie basic knots useful in boating and diving. Good knots to know include the square, figure eight, and bowline knots. The one knot missing from this book is how to properly secure a line to a cleat. This can be found in *Piloting, Seamanship, and Small Boat Handling.*

21. **Lewis, John E., Ph.D. and Shreeves, Karl W.:** *Decompression Theory, Dive Tables and Dive Computers, Second Edition,* International PADI, Inc., Santa Ana, CA, 1993, 90-061228. This book covers decompression theory and reviews various computer models.

22. **Loyst, Ken:** *Dive Computers, A Consumer's Guide to History, Theory, and Performance,* Watersport Publications, Inc. San Diego, CA; 1991. 90-71911. This book covers decompression theory and reviews various computer models.

23. **Maas, Terry:** *Blue Water Hunting and Freediving,* Blue Water Freedivers, Ventura, CA 1995. Excellent book that thoroughly covers freedive spearfishing, particularly for big bluewater fish.

24. **Maloney, Elbert S.:** *Piloting, Seamanship, and Small Boat Handling,* (Commonly referred to as "Chapman's"), Hearst Marine Books, New York, NY, 1992 (and later). This is the premier text on boating and seamanship. Studying this book and practicing the techniques that it presents provides a good foundation for becoming a proficient captain, crew, and guest. Studying the entire book is recommended but a good start includes chapters: 1) Nautical Terms, 6) Small Boat Seamanship, 7) Power Cruiser Seamanship, 11) Anchoring, 12) Safety Afloat, 13) Marlinespike Seamanship.

25. **O'Keefe, M. Timothy and Larsen, Larry:** *Fish & Dive Florida and The Keys,* Larsen's Outdoor Publishing, Lakeland, FL, 1992. Good guide on fishing and diving in Florida.

26. **Resdeck, John, Jr.:** *SCUBA Safe and Simple,* Simon & Schuster, Inc., New York, NY, 1990. This book provides a good overall discussion of diving technique, equipment, and specialties, including spearfishing. It contains "un-tempered for the diving market place" viewpoints of such topics as breath hold diving and dangerous underwater marine life.

27. **SCUBA Sun & Fun, Inc.:** *Tail Tamer,* Lake Orion, MI, 1992, (800)336-8245. This fifty-three minute color video shows how to catch and clean lobster (Florida).

28. **Sheckler, Dale and Kim:** *Southern California's Best Beach Dives,* California Diving News, 1994, (310)792-2333. As the name indicates, this book provides a list of California beach dives with descriptions.

29. **Sheckler, Dale:** *Successful Underwater Hunting and Gathering, California Edition,* California Diving News, 1994, (310)792-2333. This book serves as a good California underwater hunting reference. It covers fish, lobster, abalone, rock scallops, prismo clams, and urchins.

30. **Slosky, Bill and Walker, Art:** *Guide to the Underwater,* Bonanza Books Division of Crown Publications, NY. MCMLXVI. Book devoted to free diving and free diving activities. This book includes a chapter on spearfishing (Phase 3) and represents one of the earliest published applications of filters and flash to provide true color underwater photography.

31. **Stearns, Walt:** "Sharks & Divers," *Sport Diver Magazine,* Winter Park, FL, Preview Issue, 1994. Article reviewing various theories on shark encounters with divers and describing the species most commonly seen by divers.

32. **Stebbins, Rod and Susie:** *Coastal Loran Coordinates, Volumes I Texas to Maine, Volume II Pacific Coast, Volume III, Great Lakes,* International Marine Publishing, Blue Ridge Summit, PA, 1990, (800)822-8158. LORAN and latitude and longitude coordinates of ports, anchorages, ledges, wrecks, reefs, and fishing spots.

33. **Wheeler, Alwyne:** *Fishes of the World,* MacMillan Publishing Col, Inc., New York, NY, 1975. This illustrated dictionary of fish includes line drawings and detailed descriptions of species. It discusses distribution, habitat, habits, and life cycle.